MACARONI AND CHEESE

Macaroni and Cheese

52 RECIPES, FROM SIMPLE TO SUBLIME

Joan Schwartz

VILLARD (V) NEW YORK

All rights reserved under International and Pan-American Copyright Conventions.
Published in the United States by Villard Books, a division of Random House, Inc.,
New York, and simultaneously in Canada by Random House of Canada Limited, Toronto.

Villard Books is a registered trademark of Random House, Inc.
Colophon is a trademark of Random House, Inc.

Grateful acknowledgment is made to the following for permission
to reprint previously published material:

Simon & Schuster, Inc.: Adaptation of "Today's Mac and Cheese" from
Salsas That Cook, by Rick Bayless. Copyright © 1998 by Richard Lane Bayless.
Adapted with the permission of Scribner, a division of Simon & Schuster, Inc.

Workman Publishing Company, Inc.: "Dad Page's Macaroni and Cheese" excerpted from
Taste of Home, by Barbara Shinn and David Page. Copyright © 2001 by Barbara Shinn
and David Page. All rights reserved. Used by permission of Artisan, a division of
Workman Publishing Company, Inc., New York.

LIBRARY OF CONGRESS CATALOGING-IN-PUBLICATION DATA
Schwartz, Joan.
Macaroni and cheese : 52 recipes, from simple to sublime / Joan Schwartz.
p.   cm.
ISBN 0-375-75700-7
1. Cookery (Pasta)   I. Title.
TX809.M17 S27   2001
641.8'22—dc21   2001023536

Villard Books website: www.villard.com

Printed in the United States of America on acid-free paper

4 6 8 9 7 5 3

BOOK DESIGN BY BARBARA M. BACHMAN

To my all-time favorite dining companions:

Allen, David, Rachel, and Deborah

This book began with an inspired suggestion from my agent, Stacey Glick, of Jane Dystel Literary Management. Thanks to Stacey for planting and nurturing the idea and to Jane, as always, for her support and wisdom.

I am grateful to my editor, Pamela Cannon, who fueled the creative process with her enthusiasm and expertise.

A star-studded cast of chefs (whose biographies comprise the last part of the book) contributed inspiration and hard work, along with consistent good cheer. To all, old friends and new, my boundless gratitude.

I am especially indebted to Eve Lindenblatt, who expertly tested the recipes and shared her insights, skill, and delight.

Contents

The Classic Dish

13

International Mac 43

Mac and Cheese Today

MACARONI AND CHEESE

PART 1

Introducing Mac and Cheese

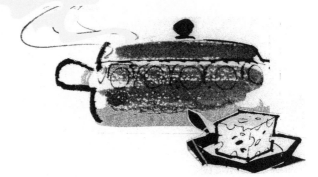

Macaroni and cheese is my kind of dish! For something so simple at heart, it is amazingly receptive to flights of fancy. It's fun to eat and it makes people happy—always. A good Mac is defined by top-quality ingredients far more than by the cook's experience or patience, and serving it will enhance your reputation as a savvy chef, caring spouse or parent, and intuitive host.

You may notice the use of superlatives throughout *Macaroni and Cheese.* The variations I have collected are sensational, awesome, seductive, wild, and, of course, supremely comforting. With Mac and Cheese, there are many world's-best recipes.

And there are very few losers in the genre. I was disappointed by a take-out portion from a food market (albeit a pricey food market) and didn't include the recipe here, but I ate every bit. It was not as good as some and that sent it to the bottom of my list; however, "bad" does not apply.

A savory, creamy, aromatic Mac is welcome as an entrée or side dish at brunch, lunch, or dinner; and sweet, puddinglike versions make great desserts. For the center of your buffet table, you couldn't do better than a gorgeous pastitsio, a multicolored terrine, or a sparkling pasta and cheese salad. Leftovers, if there are any, will rapidly disappear from the kitchen.

In assembling these recipes, I was struck over and over by the way gifted chefs approached the classic dish, respecting and changing it at the same time. All these classics and transformations start with pasta and cheese, but the results are original to each and every one.

We all grew up on macaroni and cheese and it seems that our ancestors may have done so, too, since pasta in some form was known to the ancient Greeks, Romans, and Etruscans. It was cooked in Sicily as early as the twelfth century, and Renaissance Italians enjoyed recipes that called for combining *maccheroni* with pecorino or caciocavallo cheese. Historian Stefano Milioni writes that eighteenth-century Neapolitans could stroll to the local inn and feast on a dish of macaroni with cheese for a tab of about two cents.

Pasta finally arrived in England in the eighteenth century, and from there, it soon made its way to our shores, where the early colonists prepared boiled noodles with a sort of cream and cheese sauce. Thomas Jefferson lent his considerable influence to the cause when he brought a pasta machine home from Italy in 1787 and began serving his guests at Monticello "Macaroni Pie," an early version of our very own beloved dish.

In our time, macaroni and cheese has proved itself an enduring favorite, and when we crave comfort foods, we welcome it as the most comforting of the lot. Moreover, the basic combination of cheese and pasta presents a blank slate for the imaginative cook—it offers both nostalgia and inspiration.

THE BASICS

When you cook up this perfect union of contrasting flavors and textures, keep in mind two rules for success:

Start with the best ingredients. Cheese determines the flavor of the dish, and pasta gives it a satisfying chewiness. Mediocre cheese and flabby pasta are not worth your time.

Keep the ingredients in proportion so that each stands out. Too much cheese will overwhelm, while too much pasta will give you a heavy, dense concoction. If crumb topping is part of the recipe, sprinkle on just enough to add a touch of crispness to each mouthful; it will beautifully accent the contrasts.

Look for pasta made from durum semolina, a coarse-milled hard wheat that is high in gluten; it will be sturdy enough to hold up to the cooking that Mac and Cheese requires. The best pasta has been slowly dried and has a slightly rough surface to help absorb the sauce. It should taste good on its own, with a noticeable flavor of the fine wheat that it is made from. But poor-quality pastas, or those made from soft wheat, will be bland in flavor and mushy in texture, and they will reveal their inferiority as soon as they hit the boiling water and turn it cloudy. Chef Alan Tardi (Rigatoni al Forno) recommends artisanal pastas, preferably the Martelli, Rustichella, and Lattini brands, available at specialty shops or through the Internet (see Sources), with commercial Italian pastas such as De Cecco and Del Verde acceptable as second choices.

Americans overwhelmingly choose elbow macaroni for their Mac and Cheese, but any other short, tubular dried pasta can be used, as well as imaginative variations such as butterflies, seashells, and "little ears." Chef Jody Adams's Baked Stuffed Pasta Spirals is based upon sheets of fresh pasta, and my traditional Sweet Noodle and Cheese Kugel is made with egg noodles. Each shape and kind will absorb and contrast with the cheese in its own way, lending subtle variations of texture and chewiness.

AL DENTE

These magic words describe pasta that is cooked until tender but still slightly "firm to the tooth." Chefs differ in their suggested cooking times, and package directions for each brand may vary a bit more. A good rule of thumb is to test for doneness after the shortest cooking time given: if instructions (from the chef or manufacturer) call for 8 to 10 minutes, pop a noodle in your mouth after 8 minutes—it should be al dente, or close to that state. Chefs Loren Falsone and Eric Moshier (Baked Cellentani with Four Cheeses, Prosciutto, Artichoke Hearts, and Portobellos) suggest that you stop cooking the pasta 1 minute earlier than the package directions require; and Mitchell Davis (Tomatoey Mac and Cheese) opts for 2 or 3 minutes less than the package directions. Ultimately, your own taste rules, and if you prefer pasta on the soft side, by all means go for a longer initial boil. Just remember that there may be more oven or stove-top time to come.

Cook pasta in a large pot of boiling water, about 6 quarts for 1 pound, with 1 tablespoon of salt. Don't cover the pot, and stir occasionally to make sure the pasta does not stick.

The generic "mac" or "macaroni" in the recipe titles refers to a specific shape in each recipe. Start with that shape and then experiment, if you like, using the options below. Four cups, or 1 pound, of dry pasta will yield 8 cups cooked; 1 pound of egg noodles will yield 7 cups cooked.

Bucatini:	long macaroni tubes
Cavatelli:	small, curly-edged shells
Cavatappi or elbow twists:	tubular corkscrew or spiral shapes
Cellentani:	ridged twisted tubes
Conchiglie:	conch shells
Baby shells:	small conchiglie
Ditali, ditalini, "thimbles":	short, smooth tubes
Ditali ligati:	tiny ditali
Egg noodles:	flat, long pasta made with eggs
Elbow macaroni:	short, curved tubes
Short macaroni:	small elbows
Farfalle:	butterflies or bow ties
Farfalline:	tiny farfalle
Fusilli:	corkscrews
Garganelli:	ridged egg pasta, rolled into thin tubes
Mezzani:	tubular, about 1¼ inches long; thicker than elbows
Orecchiette:	little ears
Pastina, "tiny dough":	very small five-pointed stars made with eggs
Penne:	quills, cut diagonally

Penne rigate:	ridged penne
Radiatore, "radiators":	small, ruffled, ridged tubes
Rigatoni:	1½-inch-wide ridged tubes
Mezza rigatoni:	smaller ridged tubes
Rotelle, "wagon wheels":	small wheel shapes
Rotini:	little corkscrews
Ziti, "bridegrooms":	straight-cut narrow tubes

CHEESES

Although the classic Mac and Cheese brings to mind the flavors of American and Cheddar cheeses, there are endless varieties that will melt beautifully to enrobe your pasta. They may be made from cow's, sheep's, or goat's milk; their flavors may be mild, savory, or sharp; and their textures may run the gamut from soft and semisoft to semihard and hard. Your choices are wide, but not limitless: Chef Katy Sparks (Macaroni with Many Cheeses in a Red Chile–Herb Crust) counsels that any overly aromatic type, such as Limburger, is best avoided.

While some chefs emphasize the flavor of one extraordinary cheese, such as Cheddar (John DeLucie, Mac and Cheese Soho Grand), Manchego (Allen Susser, Macaroni and Manchego), American (Wylie DuFresne, Ten-Minute Mac and Cheese), or Roquefort (Waldy Malouf, Penne with Roquefort), others combine a mild and a sharp, such as Gruyère and Cheddar (Ilene Rosen, City Bakery Macaroni and Cheese). Still others build on a variety of flavors, such as robiola, Taleggio, fontina, and Gorgonzola (Don Pintabona, Farfalle al Quattro Formaggi), or Cheddar, Asiago, and fontina (Keith Dresser, Baked Four-Cheese Pasta). Many of the baked dishes are topped with a grated hard cheese such as Parmesan.

A WORD ABOUT PARMESAN: You will find that both the generic cheese and the superior Parmigiano-Reggiano are called for in these recipes. You won't go wrong using the best you can find and grating it fresh.

Determining amounts: Each ¼ pound of hard cheese, such as Cheddar or Parmigiano-Reggiano, will yield about 1 cup grated. Each ¼ pound of softer cheese, such as Swiss, will yield about

1 cup shredded. Each $^1/_4$ pound of Roquefort will yield about 1 cup crumbled. Each $^1/_2$ pound of ricotta or cottage cheese equals 1 cup.

The following cheeses may be used in our recipes:

American:	pasteurized processed cow's milk cheese; excellent for melting
Appenzeller:	cow's milk; tangy
Asiago (Italy):	aged, semisoft cow's milk; mild, sweet flavor; loose texture; irregular holes
Asiago (Wisconsin):	cow's milk; hard cheese; mildly tangy flavor
Bel Paese:	cow's milk; mild, semisoft; excellent melting cheese
Blue cheese:	cow's or sheep's milk; aromatic and often strongly flavored; blue or green veins
Brie:	cow's milk; soft-ripened, creamy, tangy; soft, edible rind
Cabrales:	mixed cow's, goat's, and sheep's milk; creamy semisoft blue cheese with peppery, not overly salty flavor
Caciocavallo:	cow's milk; mild, a bit salty; firm texture when young; when aged, stronger flavor and good for grating
Camembert:	cow's milk; mild, rich, creamy, soft-ripened; soft, edible rind
Cantal:	cow's milk; smooth, semifirm texture; mellow flavor
Cheddar:	cow's milk; firm texture; white to pale yellow or yellow-orange; can be mild, sharp, or extra-sharp, depending upon how long it is aged
Chèvre:	goat's milk; soft, flaky; white rind; mild flavor that gets sharper with age
Comté:	cow's milk; hard but creamy; sweet and piquant flavor; similar to Gruyère

Cottage:	cow's milk; creamy, moist curds; mild flavor
Cream cheese:	cow's milk; smooth, spreadable; mild flavor
Dry Jack:	see Monterey Jack
Emmentaler:	cow's milk; mild, nutlike flavor; firm texture; holes
Feta:	sheep's or goat's milk; soft, rindless; white, salty, tangy
Fontina:	semifirm; rich, nutty flavor; pale gold; small holes
Gorgonzola:	cow's milk; rich, savory, pungent; blue-green veins
Gorgonzola Dolce, Dolcelatte:	cow's milk; soft and melting, sweet; blue veins
Gouda:	cow's milk; semihard; smooth and buttery
Grana Padano:	partially skimmed cow's milk; sharp flavor; granular quality; ideal for grating
Gruyère:	cow's milk; hard or semihard Swiss, with small holes; nutlike flavor; classic for cooking and melting
Kashkaval:	sheep's milk; firm, mildly olivelike flavor
Kasseri:	sheep's milk, semihard; mild flavor, salted with brine and aged six months
Kefalotyri:	sheep's milk; pale yellow; hard, mildly salty; good for grating; similar to pecorino
Manchego:	sheep's milk, semifirm; mild, slightly salty, nutlike flavor
Mascarpone:	cow's milk; double cream; rich, buttery, similar to cream cheese
Monterey Jack:	cow's milk; distant relative of Cheddar. Unaged has mild flavor; semisoft texture. Aged, or dry (Dry Jack), has firm texture; sharp flavor; good for grating.
Mozzarella:	cow's milk, made from stretched curds; milky flavor and color; soft, perfect for melting
Parmesan:	cow's milk; hard; perfect for grating

Parmigiano-Reggiano:	cow's milk; complex nutlike flavor; perfect for grating. Strictly controlled, it can be made only from April through November and must be aged for eighteen months.
Pecorino:	sheep's milk; tangy, peppery; hard, granular, perfect for grating
Raclette:	cow's milk; nutlike flavor; semifirm texture with small holes
Ricotta:	sheep's milk; fresh, slightly salty, soft curds; similar in texture to cottage cheese
Robiola:	cow's milk; fresh, mild and creamy; aged, nutlike, pungent
Roquefort:	sheep's milk; rich, pungent; blue veins
Swiss:	cow's milk; nutlike flavor; firm texture; large holes
Taleggio:	cow's milk; pungent, meaty, nutty, slightly salty, soft-ripened, runny, fruit nuances
Velveeta:	pasteurized prepared cheese product, good for melting

A FINAL NOTE: The major cheese manufacturers have come to the aid of Mac and Cheese lovers in a hurry. For spur-of-the-moment Macs, sealed bags of grated Cheddar, Swiss, and mixed cheeses are available in the dairy case of your supermarket or health food store, usually in 2-cup sizes. They can't be beaten for efficiency, and their quality is equal to that of other packaged cheeses.

CRISP TOPPINGS

Crumbs of some sort provide a textural counterpoint in baked Mac and Cheese and round off the dish perfectly. Every mouthful should have a bit of delicious crunch. To enhance browning, you may place the finished Mac under the broiler briefly, but watch carefully—toppings can burn fast.

FRESH BREAD CRUMBS: Make them in your food processor or blender, using slightly dry or day-old bread. One slice yields about $1/2$ cup of coarse crumbs. If you dry the bread first in a low oven, 1 slice will yield about $1/4$ cup of fine crumbs.

TOASTED BREAD CRUMBS: Spread fresh bread crumbs evenly on a baking sheet and toast in a 300°F oven for about 15 minutes.

SEASONED BREAD CRUMBS: Toss each cup of bread crumbs with $1/2$ teaspoon salt and a few grindings of pepper. You may purchase Italian seasoned crumbs or add dried oregano and basil to taste to your own toasted crumbs.

PANKO: Large, coarse, irregular-size Japanese bread crumbs, available in many supermarkets and Asian markets.

CORN BREAD CRUMBS: Make them in your food processor or blender from your favorite homemade or purchased corn bread. Use fresh, or toast as you would regular bread crumbs.

TORTILLA CRUMBS: Process tortilla chips in the food processor or blender. Fourteen to 15 tortilla chips will yield about 3 cups of crumbs.

CRACKER CRUMBS: Seven to 10 Ritz or similar crackers will yield $1/4$ to $1/3$ cup of crumbs.

BÉCHAMEL

Although traditional Mac and Cheese depends on just that—macaroni and cheese (see, for example, Wylie DuFresne, Ten-Minute Mac and Cheese; Henry Archer Meer, City Hall Mac and Cheese; Allen Susser, Macaroni and Manchego)—many recipes will have you stir the cheese into a silken béchamel before combining it with the noodles. This smooth white sauce is made quickly by melting butter and whisking in flour and milk, but you will see that each chef provides his or her own spin on both ingredients and method (Kevin Johnson, for example, makes his sauce with canola oil, for Baked Macaroni with White

Cheddar Cheese and Cremini Mushrooms). It's worthwhile to follow their recipes; you will become a béchamel expert in a very short time.

The general rule, of course, is to use a pan or baking dish large enough to hold the macaroni and cheese mixture comfortably; it may be deep or shallow, depending upon the chef's directions or your preference. The sizes I give are approximate. You may also use individual gratin dishes or ramekins, usually six to eight per pound of pasta.

For 1 to $1^1/_2$ pounds of macaroni, use a 9 by 13-inch pan that holds 15 cups; or a 3- to $3^1/_2$-quart deep baking dish.

For $^1/_2$ pound of macaroni, use an 8 by 8-inch pan that holds 8 cups; or a 9 by 9-inch pan that holds 10 cups.

Please remember these rules, which apply to all our recipes.

Butter is always unsalted.

Flour is always all-purpose, unless another type (such as Wondra) is specified.

Eggs are always large.

Milk is always whole, unless evaporated milk is specified.

Salt is always kosher or coarse.

Pepper is always freshly ground or cracked; black unless otherwise specified.

PART 2

The Classic Dish

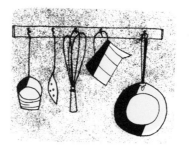

When you find yourself daydreaming about Mac and Cheese, chances are it will be one of the versions offered in this chapter. These are traditional American recipes relying on the primary ingredients: pasta, familiar cheeses, and perhaps tomatoes or onions. This is the place to do your Mac and Cheese research, as it features crisp-crusted baked versions as well as a creamy one quickly made on the stovetop and helps you to master béchamel—the cheese-infused white sauce—or to forgo it entirely.

Here are the versions we know best as pure comfort food, easily put together and guaranteed to satisfy. Creations by Matthew Kenney, Mitchel London, John DeLucie, Ilene Rosen, Barbara Shinn and David Page, Fairway Market's Michael O'Neill, Keith Dresser, José Arturo Molina, and Ira Freehof (of Comfort Diner fame) are luxurious cheese and béchamel combinations that characterize the Macs of our dreams. Think rich, creamy, smooth, cheesy, chewy, savory, and mouthwatering.

They are followed by some kitchen treasures that combine cheese and pasta without the extra step of making a béchamel (some say they are the purest versions). Henry Archer Meer's City Hall Mac and Cheese is simple and sophisticated; Wylie DuFresne's Ten-Minute Mac and Cheese relies on that palate pleaser, American cheese, in a magically quick stovetop dish; and my Simple Mac and Cheese for Two requires minimal time. Memory speaks in Mitchell Davis's Tomatoey Mac and Cheese and Joyce Wilder's Mom's Mac and Cheese with Tomatoes (both come to us courtesy of actual moms); while Leslie Holley-McKen takes us back to the Queens of her childhood, where macaroni and cheese was a special Sunday-night treat.

Mac and Cheddar Salad will help you cool down without forgetting your roots, although it is not quite as traditional as some of the other dishes here. Heaped in a sparkling crystal bowl and glittering with chunks of colorful, crisp vegetables and fresh cheese, it makes a beautiful addition to a summer party. (For a Greek macaroni salad with feta cheese, see Part 3.)

That's the starting lineup, so don't wait any longer—pick a Mac (or several) and dig in!

Macaroni with Wisconsin Asiago

Mild, slightly tangy Wisconsin Asiago is a cheese of excellent quality, and it adds special flavor and character to this dish. The creamy combination of Asiago and Cheddar is a favorite at Matthew's ultrastylish yet homey New York restaurant, Canteen.

7 tablespoons butter, plus extra for the gratin dishes	Freshly ground pepper
1 pound cavatelli	2 cups ($^{1}/_{2}$ pound) grated aged Wisconsin Asiago cheese
$^{1}/_{4}$ cup plus 2 tablespoons flour	1 cup ($^{1}/_{4}$ pound) grated sharp white Cheddar cheese
1 quart whole milk	$1^{1}/_{3}$ cups (about $5^{1}/_{2}$ ounces) grated Parmigiano-Reggiano cheese
2 teaspoons dry mustard	$^{3}/_{4}$ cup coarsely chopped flat-leaf parsley
$^{1}/_{8}$ teaspoon cayenne pepper	$^{1}/_{3}$ cup minced fresh chives
Dash of Tabasco	1 cup panko (Japanese bread crumbs)
1 tablespoon Worcestershire sauce	
Kosher salt	

1. Preheat the oven to 350°F. Butter six individual gratin dishes.

2. Bring a large pot of salted water to a boil over high heat and cook the pasta until al dente, 10 to 12 minutes. Drain and cool.

3. In a medium saucepan over moderately low heat, melt 6 tablespoons of the butter. Add the flour and cook, stirring, 3 minutes. Whisk in the milk and raise the heat to high. When the milk begins to

boil, reduce the heat to medium and cook, whisking occasionally, until thickened. Add the mustard, cayenne, Tabasco, and Worcestershire and season with salt and pepper.

4. In a large bowl, toss together the pasta, sauce, Asiago, Cheddar, 1 cup of the Parmigiano-Reggiano, the parsley, and chives. Spoon into the buttered gratin dishes. Mix together the bread crumbs and the remaining Parmigiano-Reggiano and sprinkle over the pasta. Dot lightly with the remaining butter and bake on the middle shelf until the crumbs are lightly browned and the sauce is bubbling, 25 to 30 minutes.

London Mac and Cheese

The creations from Mitchel London Foods always have unique richness and depth of flavor. Mitchel is happy to share his macaroni and cheese secrets.

TO MAKE PERFECT BÉCHAMEL: After mixing butter and flour over medium heat to make the roux, remove the pan from the heat and add hot milk all at once, whisking so there are no lumps. Always add hot milk to hot roux.

FOR THE TOMATO TOPPING VARIATION: Never use sun-dried tomatoes—they will be all you can taste. Instead, use fresh plum tomatoes, roasted at a very low temperature to concentrate their flavor but retain their texture and subtlety.

FOR THE BREAD CRUMBS: Use only fresh crumbs for the best texture.

3 cups (¾ pound) grated white sharp Cheddar cheese

1 cup (¼ pound) grated Parmigiano-Reggiano cheese, or substitute Grana Padano or pecorino cheese

1 pound ziti, penne, or short macaroni

3¾ cups whole milk

8 tablespoons butter, plus extra for the baking dish

6 tablespoons flour

½ teaspoon cayenne pepper

Small pinch of freshly grated nutmeg

Kosher salt

Freshly ground white pepper

½ cup heavy cream

½ cup fresh bread crumbs

1. Preheat the oven to 350°F. In a mixing bowl, combine the two cheeses and reserve.
2. Bring a large pot of salted water to a boil over high heat and cook the pasta until al dente, 10 to 12 minutes. Drain and place in a mixing bowl.

3. In a small saucepan over medium-high heat, bring the milk to a simmer.

4. In a large saucepan over medium heat, melt the butter; when it starts to bubble, whisk in the flour. Cook, stirring, for 5 to 6 minutes and then remove from the heat (this is the roux). Whisk in the hot milk all at once. Add the cayenne, nutmeg, and salt and pepper to taste. Return the mixture to high heat and cook, stirring, until it comes to a boil and thickens, 2 to 3 minutes.

5. Reduce the heat to low. Add 2 cups of the combined cheeses to the milk mixture and cook, stirring, until the cheeses have melted completely. Pour the sauce over the pasta in the bowl and mix lightly.

6. Lightly butter a 3 1/2-quart deep baking dish and sprinkle 1/2 cup of the combined cheeses over the bottom. Cover with one third of the pasta and one third of the remaining cheese. Repeat the layers twice, ending with a layer of cheese. Pour the cream over all, and sprinkle with the bread crumbs. Place on the middle shelf of the oven and bake until the macaroni is bubbling and the crumbs are golden brown, about 30 minutes.

VARIATION: Pour on the cream, top with a layer of oven-roasted tomatoes, and sprinkle with the bread crumbs. Bake as usual.

TO ROAST THE TOMATOES

6 to 8 plum tomatoes, halved

Olive oil for greasing the baking sheet and drizzling over the tomatoes

Kosher salt

Freshly ground pepper

Four to 6 hours before you will use the tomatoes, preheat the oven to 250°F. Arrange the tomatoes cut side up on a lightly oiled baking sheet, sprinkle with salt and pepper, and drizzle with olive oil. Roast until they are dried but still soft, 4 to 6 hours, depending upon their size (smaller tomatoes will take less time).

Mac and Cheese Soho Grand

MAKES 4 SERVINGS

A respected food writer chatting on-line about Mac and Cheese revealed: "The best I've had anywhere is in the restaurant in New York's Soho Grand Hotel." Here is the recipe, tracked down for you!

Chef DeLucie's advice: All ingredients should be the best you can buy—especially the Cheddar.

½ pound cavatappi, or substitute any short, curved pasta

2 cups whole milk

2 tablespoons butter, plus extra for the pan

1 cup (½ to ⅔ pound) finely diced onion

2 tablespoons flour

2 cups (½ pound) grated sharp Cheddar cheese, 2 tablespoons reserved

2 teaspoons Dijon mustard

⅛ teaspoon freshly grated nutmeg

Dash of Tabasco

Kosher salt

Freshly ground pepper

2 tablespoons grated Parmesan cheese

19

1. Bring a large pot of salted water to a boil over high heat and cook the pasta until al dente, 8 to 10 minutes. Drain and place in a mixing bowl.

2. Preheat the oven to 350°F. In a small saucepan over medium heat, scald the milk.

3. In a sauté pan over medium-high heat, melt the butter and cook the onion until soft and fragrant but not colored, about 3 minutes. Reduce the heat to low, add the flour, and cook, stirring, about 3 minutes. Whisk in the scalded milk, 2 cups of the Cheddar, the mustard, nutmeg, and Tabasco. Keep-

ing it over low heat, simmer, whisking occasionally, until the cheese is melted and smooth. Taste, and season with salt and pepper, if needed. Pour the mixture over the pasta and mix well.

4. Spoon the cavatappi mixture into a lightly buttered 2-quart gratin dish and sprinkle with the reserved 2 tablespoons of Cheddar and the Parmesan. Bake on the middle shelf until bubbling and browned on top, 25 to 30 minutes, and serve immediately.

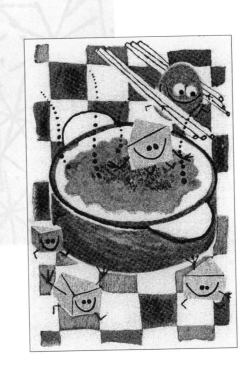

City Bakery Macaroni and Cheese

MAKES 4 TO 6 SERVINGS

The trick is in the proportions of crisp topping, creamy sauce, and smooth pasta—and Chef Rosen gets it exactly right. She advises that you have some freedom in choosing your pan: just remember that a large, flat pan will give you a greater area of crumb topping than a small, deep one.

6 tablespoons butter, plus extra for the baking dish	Kosher salt
1/4 cup corn bread crumbs (or more, depending upon pan size)	Freshly ground pepper
	1 1/4 cups (5 ounces) grated Gruyère cheese
1 pound elbow macaroni	1 1/4 cups (5 ounces) grated mild white Cheddar cheese
1 quart whole milk	
6 tablespoons flour	1 1/4 cups (5 ounces) grated Grana Padano or Parmesan cheese

1. Preheat the oven to 350°F. Lightly butter a 3 1/2-quart deep baking dish or a 9 by 13-inch baking pan.

2. Spread the crumbs in a single layer on a baking sheet and bake until golden brown, 10 to 15 minutes. Set aside.

3. Bring a large pot of salted water to a boil and cook the macaroni until al dente, 8 to 10 minutes. Drain and place in a large bowl. (To prepare up to a day ahead, mix in a small amount of canola oil, cover with plastic wrap, and refrigerate until ready to use.)

4. Bring the milk to a simmer in a small saucepan over medium-high heat.

5. In a medium saucepan over medium-low heat, melt the 6 tablespoons of butter, add the flour, and mix well with a wooden spoon or spatula. Cook, stirring, for 3 minutes. Whisk in the hot milk and

continue whisking until smooth. Raise the heat to medium and cook, stirring continuously, until the mixture thickens enough to coat the spoon. Season with salt and pepper and strain through a fine strainer.

6. Add the sauce to the cooked macaroni. Add 1 cup each of the Gruyère, Cheddar, and Grana Padano and mix well. Taste, and season with salt and pepper if necessary.

7. Pour the macaroni mixture into the baking dish and sprinkle with the remaining cheese. (At this point, the macaroni and cheese may be cooled on the counter, covered, and refrigerated for one day. Before proceeding, preheat the oven to 350°F.)

8. Sprinkle the toasted corn bread crumbs evenly over the casserole and cover with foil. Bake on the middle shelf until heated through, about 20 minutes; remove the foil and continue baking until the top is golden brown, an additional 10 minutes. Allow to stand for 10 minutes before serving.

Food for the Family

Dad Page's Macaroni and Cheese

MAKES 2 TO 4 SERVINGS

Barbara and David, the guiding spirits of Home Restaurant and Shinn Vineyard, like to keep their macaroni and cheese similar to the childhood dish that inspires many happy memories. With the sweet underlying flavors of onion and garlic and the freshness of herbs, this is a true classic.

4 tablespoons butter, plus extra for the pans	1 teaspoon freshly ground pepper
1 pound elbow macaroni	3/4 cup (3 ounces) grated extra-sharp Cheddar cheese
1 large (about 3/4 pound) yellow onion, cut into 1/8-inch dice	3/4 cup (3 ounces) grated Wisconsin Asiago cheese
1 tablespoon minced garlic	3/4 cup (3 ounces) grated Dry Jack cheese
3 tablespoons flour	2 plum tomatoes, sliced
4 cups whole milk	1/2 cup seasoned bread crumbs
1 teaspoon mild paprika	1 tablespoon chopped fresh parsley
1/2 teaspoon freshly grated nutmeg	1 tablespoon chopped fresh thyme
2 teaspoons kosher salt	1 tablespoon chopped fresh chives

1. Preheat the oven to 400°F. Butter two 6-inch cast-iron skillets or one 12-inch skillet.

2. Bring a large pot of salted water to a boil over high heat and cook the macaroni until al dente, 8 to 10 minutes. Drain and place in a large bowl.

3. Melt the 4 tablespoons of butter in a large pot over medium heat. Add the onion and garlic and cook until they are softened, about 2 minutes. Whisk in the flour and cook, stirring constantly, until the mixture turns light brown, about 3 minutes. Gradually whisk in the milk. Add the paprika, nutmeg,

salt, and pepper. Reduce the heat to low and cook, stirring, until the sauce is thickened, about 5 minutes. Add the cheeses and stir until they are melted. Add the macaroni and stir until the noodles are thoroughly coated. Remove from the heat.

4. Transfer the macaroni mixture to the buttered skillets. Top with the sliced tomatoes. Sprinkle the bread crumbs on top.

5. Bake until the cheese is bubbling and golden brown, about 30 minutes. Garnish with the chopped herbs.

Fairway Market Mac and Cheese

The basic dish matures into upscale comfort food with the addition of Comté, a superlative Gruyère. A favorite of Fairway's cosmopolitan customers, it is creamy and fabulous.

2 tablespoons butter, plus extra for the pan

1 pound elbow macaroni (preferably De Cecco)

2 tablespoons flour

3 cups half-and-half

4 cups (1 pound) shredded extra-sharp Wisconsin Cheddar cheese

2 cups (½ pound) shredded French Comté cheese

Kosher salt

Freshly ground white pepper

2 tablespoons plain bread crumbs

1. Preheat the oven to 350°F. Generously butter a 9 by 13-inch baking pan.

2. Bring a large pot of salted water to a boil over high heat and cook the macaroni until al dente, 8 to 10 minutes. Drain and place in a large bowl.

3. In a large pot over medium heat, melt the 2 tablespoons of butter. Whisk in the flour, mixing well so there are no lumps. Slowly whisk in the half-and-half, raise the heat to medium-high, and bring the mixture to a boil. Add the cheeses, reduce the heat to medium, and whisk well to incorporate. Season with salt and pepper.

4. Add the sauce to the macaroni and mix well to combine.

5. Transfer the macaroni mixture to the baking pan and sprinkle with the bread crumbs. Bake for 20 to 25 minutes, until bubbly and golden.

Baked Four-Cheese Pasta

Even before your first taste, you can tell just by the creaminess of the sauce how rich and delicious this will be. Keith advises us that this dish will taste best with freshly grated cheeses—especially Vermont Cheddar.

Bake the mixture in a deep casserole because it can easily boil over. If you decide to use a shallow pan, put it on a foil-lined baking sheet.

8 tablespoons butter, plus extra for the baking dish	2 cups (1/2 pound) grated sharp Cheddar cheese
1 pound penne	2 cups (1/2 pound) grated Asiago cheese
4 cups whole milk	2 cups (1/2 pound) grated fontina cheese
6 tablespoons flour	1 cup plain bread crumbs
1 1/2 teaspoons kosher salt	1/2 cup (2 ounces) grated Parmesan cheese
1/4 teaspoon cayenne pepper	2 tablespoons butter, melted
	1 cup heavy cream

1. Preheat the oven to 350°F. Butter a 9 by 13-inch baking dish or 2 1/2-quart casserole.
2. Bring 6 quarts of salted water to a boil. Add the pasta and cook, stirring occasionally, until al dente, 10 to 12 minutes. Drain the pasta and rinse with cold water. Drain again and place in a large bowl.
3. In a medium saucepan over medium heat, bring the milk to a boil. Remove from the heat.
4. In a medium, heavy-bottomed saucepan over medium-high heat, melt the 8 tablespoons of butter. Reduce the heat to low and whisk in the flour, cooking for 3 to 4 minutes. Be careful not to brown

the mixture. Slowly add the hot milk, whisking constantly (constant whisking will ensure that there are no lumps). Add the salt and cayenne, raise the heat to medium, and simmer, stirring constantly, until the mixture has thickened, 8 to 10 minutes.

5. Remove from the heat and add 1 cup each of the grated Cheddar, Asiago, and fontina, whisking until the cheeses are melted. Pour the cheese sauce over the pasta, tossing to coat the pasta evenly.

6. Place half of the coated pasta in the buttered baking dish and distribute the remaining grated Cheddar, Asiago, and fontina over the top. Cover with the remaining pasta.

7. In a mixing bowl, toss together the bread crumbs, Parmesan, and melted butter. Pour the heavy cream over the pasta and evenly distribute the bread crumb mixture over the top. Bake on the middle shelf until the top is light brown and the mixture is bubbling, 30 to 35 minutes.

Chat n' Chew Macaroni and Cheese

MAKES 6 TO 8 SERVINGS

Hearty and a bit spicy, this dish is a warming treat on a cold winter's evening. It is a favorite at Chat n' Chew, the comfortable downtown Manhattan restaurant where Chef Molina presides over the kitchen.

$1/2$ pound butter, plus extra for the baking dish

$1^1/4$ pounds elbow macaroni

2 cups heavy cream

2 cups whole milk

1 small ($1/4$ to $1/3$ pound) onion, diced small (about $1/2$ cup)

4 cloves garlic, minced

1 cup flour

5 cups ($1^1/4$ pounds) shredded sharp Cheddar cheese

8 slices American cheese, broken into small pieces

2 cups ($1/2$ pound) grated Parmesan cheese

3 tablespoons green Tabasco

$1/4$ teaspoon ground cumin

Kosher salt

Freshly ground pepper

$1/2$ cup seasoned bread crumbs

1. Preheat the oven to 350°F. Lightly butter a 9 by 13 by 4-inch baking dish.

2. Bring a large pot of salted water to a boil over high heat and cook the macaroni until al dente, 8 to 10 minutes. Drain.

3. In a small bowl, combine the cream and milk.

4. In a large saucepan over medium heat, melt the $1/2$ pound of butter and cook the onion and garlic until the onion is translucent, about 6 minutes, stirring occasionally. Add the flour, stirring con-

stantly for 3 minutes. Add the cream mixture in a steady stream and whisk until smooth. Bring to a boil, stirring occasionally, 8 to 10 minutes.

5. Stir in 4 cups of the Cheddar, the American cheese, 1 cup of the grated Parmesan, the Tabasco, and cumin. Stir until all the cheese has melted; the sauce will be very thick and creamy. Season with salt and pepper.

6. Remove the sauce from the heat and stir in the pasta. Pour the mixture into the prepared baking dish. Sprinkle with the remaining Cheddar, then the Parmesan, and finally the bread crumbs.

7. Bake uncovered on the middle shelf for about 20 minutes, until bubbling and brown on top.

Comfort Diner Mac and Cheese

MAKES 6 SERVINGS

Ira Freehof developed this creamy, crusty Mac for his Comfort Diners in New York, and it has become one of their most popular dishes. At home as well, it offers a lot of contentment to kids and grown-ups alike.

4 tablespoons plus 1 teaspoon butter, plus extra for the baking dish

1 pound elbow macaroni

1 tablespoon olive oil or vegetable oil

3½ cups whole milk

¼ cup flour

1 cup (¼ pound) lightly packed grated American cheese

1 cup (¼ pound) lightly packed grated Italian fontina cheese

Kosher salt

½ teaspoon freshly ground pepper

2½ teaspoons Dijon mustard

1 cup (¼ pound) shredded Cheddar cheese

½ cup fresh bread crumbs

1. Preheat the oven to 375°F. Butter a 9-inch square baking dish.

2. Bring a large pot of salted water to a boil over high heat and cook the macaroni until al dente, 8 to 10 minutes. Drain and rinse with cool water. Place in a large mixing bowl and drizzle with the oil.

3. In a small saucepan over medium-high heat, warm the milk.

4. In a large saucepan over medium-low heat, melt 4 tablespoons of the butter. Sprinkle in the flour and whisk constantly until the flour is absorbed and the mixture is bubbling gently and lightly golden, 2 to 3 minutes. Gradually add the warm milk, whisking continuously. Raise the heat to medium and bring to a simmer, stirring with a wooden spoon until smooth and slightly thickened.

5. Add the American cheese and fontina and remove the pot from the heat. Whisk the mixture until the cheese is almost completely melted; stir in the salt, pepper, and mustard. Pour the sauce over the macaroni and stir to combine. Transfer to the prepared baking dish.

6. In a small bowl, combine the shredded Cheddar and the bread crumbs, and sprinkle evenly over the macaroni. Cut the remaining teaspoon of butter into small bits and dot the casserole. Bake on the middle shelf until bubbling and a crust begins to form, 20 to 25 minutes.

City Hall Mac and Cheese

MAKES 6 TO 8 SERVINGS

American and Monterey Jack cheeses melt beautifully and give a home-style feeling to this elegant dish. The sauce, based on heavy cream and milk, is thick and rich with a hint of spiciness. Try Chef Meer's Mac on its own or as a savory accompaniment to perfectly grilled steaks, as it is served at City Hall, his Manhattan restaurant.

Butter for the pan
1 pound penne rigate
2 cups heavy cream
2 cups whole milk
1/2 teaspoon cayenne pepper
1/4 teaspoon freshly grated nutmeg
2 cups (1/2 pound) grated American cheese

1 1/3 cups (about 1/3 pound) grated Monterey Jack cheese
Kosher salt
Freshly ground pepper
1/2 cup panko (Japanese bread crumbs)
2 teaspoons chopped fresh parsley
2 teaspoons grated Parmesan cheese

1. Preheat the oven to 350°F. Butter a 9 by 13-inch baking pan.

2. Bring 6 quarts of salted water to a boil. Add the pasta and cook, stirring occasionally, until al dente, 9 to 10 minutes. Drain.

3. Combine the cream, milk, cayenne, and nutmeg in a large saucepan over medium-high heat and reduce by half, about 15 minutes. (Once the mixture starts to simmer, stir to break the layer of foam so that it will not boil over.) Reduce the heat to medium-low, add the American and Monterey Jack cheeses, and whisk until well blended. Season with salt and pepper.

4. Add the penne and stir vigorously (taking care not to break the pasta)—this will release starch and help to thicken the sauce.

5. Pour or spoon the pasta into the baking dish. Combine the panko, parsley, and Parmesan and sprinkle over the pasta. Bake until bubbly and golden, approximately 15 minutes.

Ten-Minute Mac and Cheese

Well, maybe eleven—the time depends entirely upon how long the pasta cooks. Start the cheese sauce when you put the water on to boil and it will be ready by the time the pasta is done; then combine the mezzani and sauce and ladle your creamy Mac into deep bowls. Macaroni and cheese out of a box takes longer!

Chef DuFresne, who is a purist when it comes to Mac and Cheese, prepares this minimalist classic at his downtown New York restaurant, 71 Clinton Fresh Food. He doesn't recommend adding any salt, pepper, or spices, letting the pristine flavor of American cheese carry the dish.

½ pound mezzani, or substitute penne or shells	5 teaspoons cornstarch
2 cups whole milk	2 tablespoons warm water
15 slices American cheese, broken into small pieces	¼ cup toasted bread crumbs

1. Bring 4 quarts of salted water to a boil over high heat. Add the pasta and cook until al dente, 10 to 13 minutes.

2. Meanwhile, in a large saucepan over medium-high heat, bring the milk to a boil. Whisk in the cheese, lower the heat to medium, and cook until completely melted.

3. In a small bowl or cup, dissolve the cornstarch in the water and whisk it into the milk mixture; raise the heat to medium-high and bring the mixture to a boil, whisking occasionally. Remove from the heat and continue whisking until thickened slightly.

4. When the pasta is cooked, drain it well and pour it into the pot with the sauce, stirring to combine. Divide among three or four serving bowls, sprinkle with the toasted bread crumbs, and serve.

Simple Mac and Cheese for Two

MAKES 2 SERVINGS

Easy! Quick! Painless! This is a good basic Mac. Don't expect the cheese to melt before baking—it doesn't have to.

Butter for the ramekins	Kosher salt
1 cup penne	Freshly ground pepper
1 cup half-and-half	2 tablespoons grated Parmigiano-Reggiano cheese
1 cup (¼ pound) grated Cheddar cheese	
Dash of Tabasco	

1. Preheat the oven to 350°F. Butter two 1-cup ovenproof ramekins or small baking dishes.

2. Bring a medium pot of salted water to a boil over high heat and cook the pasta until al dente, 10 to 12 minutes. Drain.

3. In a medium bowl, combine the half-and-half, Cheddar, and penne and season to taste with Tabasco, salt, and pepper. Pour into the prepared ramekins and sprinkle with the Parmigiano-Reggiano. Bake on the middle shelf until set, 15 to 20 minutes. Let rest for 5 minutes before serving.

35

THE CLASSIC DISH

Tomatoey Mac and Cheese

This baked macaroni and cheese was a staple in the Davis family while Mitchell, now James Beard Foundation executive editor and publisher, was growing up, and his mother still makes it when he comes home for dinner. Her secret is to use two kinds of Cheddar—extra-sharp and mild—and to cut it into cubes, rather than grate it.

For best results, assemble it the night before and let it sit in the fridge. That way, the noodles will absorb some of the tomato juice and the ingredients will meld together into a delicious whole.

1 pound penne

4 tablespoons butter, plus extra for the baking dish

½ pound extra-sharp Cheddar cheese, cut into ½-inch cubes

½ pound mild Cheddar cheese, cut into ½-inch cubes

1 28-ounce can whole tomatoes, roughly chopped, with their juice

2 tablespoons sugar

Pinch of kosher salt

Pinch of freshly ground pepper

1. Bring a large pot of salted water to a boil over high heat and cook the pasta until just al dente, 2 or 3 minutes less than the package directions. Drain in a colander but do not rinse.

2. Return the pasta to the pot and stir in the 4 tablespoons of butter. Add the cheeses, tomatoes, and

sugar, stir to combine, and season with the salt and pepper. Pour into a lightly buttered 2-quart rectangular baking dish (Pyrex works well). Pile high; it will hold. If you are finishing the casserole the following day, cover with plastic wrap and refrigerate overnight.

3. When you are ready to bake, preheat the oven to 375°F. Bake on the middle shelf until the top is brown and crisp and the casserole is bubbling, 40 to 45 minutes (if it has been refrigerated, cook a few minutes longer).

Mom's Mac and Cheese with Tomatoes

MAKES 4 TO 6 SERVINGS

Two recipes from the Wilder family illustrate Mac's wide range. This is the first, and it is perfectly simple and delicious (the second, Macaroni with Duck Prosciutto, Chanterelles, and Mascarpone, page 95, offers an adventurous, creative spin). According to Chef Janos Wilder, his mother Joyce's macaroni and cheese is "the world's best."

Butter for the baking dish	Kosher salt
1 pound elbow macaroni	Freshly ground pepper
1 28-ounce can whole peeled tomatoes, drained, coarsely chopped, and drained again	4 cups (1 pound) coarsely grated sharp Cheddar cheese

1. Preheat the oven to 375°F. Butter a 3-quart deep baking dish.
2. Bring a large pot of salted water to a boil over high heat and cook the pasta until al dente, 8 to 10 minutes. Drain.
3. In the baking dish, make a layer of macaroni, top with a layer of tomatoes, sprinkle lightly with salt and pepper, and top with a layer of Cheddar cheese. Repeat until all the ingredients are used, saving a few pieces of tomato to place on top of the casserole.
4. Bake on the middle shelf until browned, 40 to 45 minutes.

Queens (N.Y.) Mac and Cheese

No Sunday dinner was complete without macaroni and cheese, when New York caterer Leslie Holley-McKen was a child. In this version, based on a family recipe, the cheeses melt into a rich custardy base of evaporated milk, heavy cream, and egg, with mustard and Red Devil Sauce providing a piquant touch.

6 tablespoons butter, plus extra for the baking dish	½ pound Velveeta or American cheese, cut into ½-inch cubes
1 pound elbow macaroni	½ cup heavy cream
3 12-ounce cans evaporated milk	1 egg, lightly beaten
1 tablespoon Dijon mustard	Kosher salt
2 tablespoons Red Devil Sauce	Freshly ground pepper
4 cups (1 pound) coarsely grated sharp Cheddar cheese	1 cup panko (Japanese bread crumbs)

1. Preheat the oven to 350°F. Lightly butter a 3½-quart deep baking dish or a 9 by 13-inch baking pan.

2. Bring a large pot of salted water to a boil over high heat and cook the pasta until al dente, 8 to 10 minutes. Drain, pour into a large mixing bowl, and toss with 4 tablespoons of the butter.

3. In a small saucepan over medium heat, bring the evaporated milk to a scald and add it to the macaroni. Add the mustard, Red Devil Sauce, and Cheddar and stir well (the cheese should start to

melt). Add the Velveeta and cream and stir well. The macaroni and chunks of cheese should be swimming in the sauce. Add the egg and mix well. Season with salt, if needed, and plenty of pepper.

4. Pour into the prepared baking dish that has been placed on a sheet pan to catch spills (the baking dish will be completely full). Sprinkle with the panko and dot with the remaining 2 tablespoons of butter. Bake until golden brown and bubbling, 25 to 30 minutes.

Mac and Cheddar Salad

When you crave something cool, pasta salads are a refreshing take on our favorite combination of ingredients. This one is pure farmhouse kitchen.

1/2 pound elbow macaroni	1 stalk celery, thinly sliced
7 tablespoons olive oil	2 scallions, white and 2 inches of the green, thinly sliced
2 tablespoons fresh lemon juice or white wine vinegar	4 medium radishes, thinly sliced
Kosher salt	1 cup (1/4 pound) shredded sharp Cheddar cheese, or substitute American cheese
Freshly ground pepper	
1 small red bell pepper, seeded and julienned	

1. Bring a large pot of salted water to a boil over high heat and cook the pasta until al dente, 8 to 10 minutes. Drain, place in a large salad bowl, and toss with 1 tablespoon of the olive oil. Let cool to room temperature.

2. Combine the lemon juice with a pinch of salt, add pepper to taste, and whisk with the remaining 6 tablespoons of olive oil to make a vinaigrette.

3. Add the bell pepper, celery, scallions, radishes, and cheese to the pasta. Toss with the vinaigrette and season with salt and pepper.

PART 3

International Mac

*L*ike the recipes in Part 2, these are traditional in both ingredients and techniques, but their traditions are global rather than American. Although Italian, Greek, and French influences on pasta dishes are legendary, the international spirit isn't limited to the classics; it inspires the dishes in Part 4, "Mac and Cheese Today," and that often has made recipe placement a very close call. Consider this part a treasury of dishes that would pass muster with an Old World *nonna* or *grandmère*—who happens to be a fantastic cook.

International dishes provide an education in food, and you will see that what is customary in Greece (*ras el hanout,* Aleppo pepper) or Provence (salt cod) can be new and surprising to American macaroni gourmets. The cheeses, especially, are a departure from earlier recipes. In place of Cheddar and American, look for such delights as Manchego, robiola, Taleggio, Gorgonzola, Fontina Val d'Aosta, and kefalotyri.

Italy, the cradle of macaroni, inspires Alan Tardi's Rigatoni al Forno, Melissa Kelly's Orecchiette con Fonduta (with its fascinating sauce method), Don Pintabona's Farfalle al Quattro Formaggi, and Andrea Curto's Wish Macaroni and Cheese, as well my simple Mozzarella Mac.

Antoine Bouterin offers a memory of his Provençal childhood in Macaroni Gratin Mas Antoine, and Gordon Hamersley transports us to France with his charming cod and garlic–enriched Macaroni and Cheese Provençal.

Two Greek pasta dishes share the same spirit but are direct opposites. Nora Pouillon's Greek (and Organic) Macaroni and Cheese couples baked macaroni with an herbal, colorful Greek salad; while

James Botsacos's Pastitsio is a sturdy combination of macaroni, cheese, yogurt, meat, tomatoes, spices, and herbs. And a crisp, refreshing Macaroni and Feta Salad is a showcase of Greek flavors.

Allen Susser's Macaroni and Manchego accents Spanish Manchego cheese with tender shallots and fennel. The Swiss contribute a stick-to-the-ribs winter Swiss Mac with Potatoes; and my favorite Sweet Noodle and Cheese Kugel is an Eastern European Jewish dish passed down from generation to generation, rich with vanilla and creamy cheeses.

Rigatoni al Forno

A stellar dish, prepared for a James Beard Awards gala.

Chef Tardi, of Follonico in New York City, suggests that you can be flexible with cheeses: Gorgonzola adds a little funkiness and mozzarella gives chewiness, but feel free to use what you have in the fridge. Most important for flavor and texture, use the best-quality pasta, available at specialty food stores or over the Internet. For his specific suggestions, see page 3.

1 pound rigatoni

2 cups heavy cream, plus extra if needed

1 cup whole milk, plus extra if needed

1 small clove garlic, crushed and minced

¼ pound Gorgonzola Dolce cheese, broken into small pieces (1 cup)

1 cup (¼ pound) grated Grana Padano or Parmigiano-Reggiano cheese

½ teaspoon dried oregano or 1 teaspoon chopped fresh oregano

Freshly ground pepper

¼ pound unsalted fresh mozzarella cheese, cut into ¼-inch dice

¼ pound Fontina Val d'Aosta cheese, rind removed, cut into ¼-inch dice

Olive oil for the baking dish

2 tablespoons plain bread crumbs

1. Preheat the oven to 400°F.

2. Bring a large pot of salted water to a boil over high heat and cook the pasta until al dente, 10 to 12 minutes. Drain and place in a mixing bowl.

3. While the pasta is cooking, in a medium shallow pot or skillet (preferably stainless steel) over medium-high heat, combine the cream and milk and bring to a simmer. Add the garlic; then stir in the Gorgonzola Dolce. When the cheese has melted, add all but 1 tablespoon of the Grana Padano,

reduce the heat to medium, and cook, stirring occasionally, until the sauce is moderately thick and creamy, 10 to 12 minutes. Remove from the heat and add the oregano and pepper.

4. Pour the cream sauce over the pasta. Add the mozzarella and Fontina Val d'Aosta and mix well. The mixture should be moist and creamy; if it is too dry, add a little more milk or cream.

5. Brush the bottom and sides of a 9 by 13-inch baking dish (preferably terra-cotta) with olive oil and pour in the pasta, which should almost entirely fill the baking dish. Sprinkle with the bread crumbs and the remaining Grana Padano. Bake on the middle shelf until the sauce is bubbling and the top is golden brown and crisp, 20 to 25 minutes.

46

Orecchiette con Fonduta

MAKES 4 TO 6 SERVINGS

On a recent visit to Italy, Chef Melissa Kelly discovered Orecchiette con Fonduta, a macaroni and cheese she describes as decadent, luxurious, and *delizioso*! She added her version to the menu of her Maine restaurant, Primo, and loves to serve it when the first spring garlic and ramps (wild leeks) start popping up in the woods and perfuming the air with their wonderful scent. This is Mac and Cheese all grown-up.

½ pound fontina cheese, preferably Italian, rind removed, cut into ¼-inch cubes

2 cups whole milk

2 tablespoons butter, plus extra for the pan

1 loaf Italian or French bread, torn into large pieces

3 tablespoons extra-virgin olive oil

1 tablespoon minced garlic

Kosher salt

Freshly ground black pepper

5 egg yolks

Freshly grated nutmeg

Freshly ground white pepper

Drizzle of white truffle oil (see Sources)

1 pound orecchiette

2 shallots, minced (about ¼ cup)

4 ounces morels, thinly sliced

8 ramps (see Sources), greens separated from bulbs, both parts cut into chiffonade (thin ribbons). (If ramps are not available, you may substitute scallions, for a somewhat different flavor.)

Summer truffles, optional

1. Place the cheese in a large heat-resistant glass bowl and cover with the milk. Refrigerate, covered, for 1 hour (or up to 4); the milk will soak into the cheese.

2. Preheat the oven to 350°F. Lightly butter a 9 by 13-inch pan.

3. In a food processor, grind the bread into coarse crumbs. Place in a bowl and toss with the olive oil, garlic, and salt and black pepper to taste. Spread on a baking sheet and toast in the oven until crisp and golden brown, about 10 minutes. Reserve.

4. To make the fonduta, place a large pot of salted water over high heat and bring to a boil. Place the bowl of cheese and milk over the pot of boiling water, making sure the water does not touch the bottom of the bowl, and add the egg yolks to the bowl, whisking constantly until the cheese has melted. Season with nutmeg, white pepper, and truffle oil to taste, remove the bowl from the water, and set aside. (This can also be done in a double boiler. In that case, bring another large pot of salted water to a boil over high heat for cooking the pasta.)

5. Add the pasta to the boiling water and cook until al dente, about 10 minutes.

6. While the pasta is cooking, melt the 2 tablespoons of butter in a large saucepan over medium-high heat; when it begins to foam, add the shallots, morels, and ramp bulbs. Season with salt and black pepper and cook, stirring, until tender, 3 to 5 minutes.

7. When the pasta is done, drain and add it to the pan with the sautéed vegetables. Add the ramp tops and the fonduta, combine well, and adjust the seasoning. Pour into the prepared pan, top with the bread crumbs, and bake until the mixture bubbles and turns golden, 20 to 25 minutes. Before serving, shave the truffles over the top (as many as you dare).

Farfalle al Quattro Formaggi

MAKES 4 TO 6 SERVINGS

This mixture of flavorful Italian cheeses—creamy, soft robiola, pungent Taleggio, and rich, nutty fontina—stirred into an oniony béchamel is a winner from the chef of New York's Tribeca Grill. The buttery topping adds an extra kick of Gorgonzola. Absolutely irresistible!

1 pound farfalle, or substitute baby shells, orecchiette, or mezza rigatoni

2 cups whole milk

6 tablespoons butter, plus extra for the baking dish

1 medium onion, minced (about 1¼ cups)

¼ cup flour

2 ounces aged robiola cheese, broken into small pieces (½ cup)

¼ pound fontina cheese, broken into small pieces (1 cup)

¼ pound Taleggio cheese, broken into small pieces (1 cup)

Fresh-cracked black pepper (see Note)

2 ounces Gorgonzola cheese, crumbled (½ cup)

⅓ cup seasoned Italian bread crumbs

1. Preheat the oven to 350°F.
2. Bring a large pot of salted water to a boil over high heat and cook the pasta until al dente, 10 to 12 minutes. Drain and set aside.
3. In a small saucepan over low heat, bring the milk to a scald.
4. In a large saucepan over medium heat, melt 4 tablespoons of the butter and cook the onion until soft and fragrant, but not colored, 3 to 4 minutes. Reduce the heat to medium-low, add the flour, and cook, stirring, about 3 minutes. Add the scalded milk, raise the heat to medium, and bring to a boil. Simmer, whisking, for 3 to 5 minutes, until thickened and smooth, with chunks of onion.

5. Remove from the heat and gradually stir in the robiola, fontina, and Taleggio, in batches, until the cheeses are incorporated (they need not melt entirely). Add the pasta and stir well to combine. Season with pepper.

6. Butter a 4-quart shallow flameproof baking dish and add the pasta. Sprinkle with the Gorgonzola and the bread crumbs and dot with the remaining 2 tablespoons of butter. Bake on the middle shelf until bubbling, about 25 minutes.

7. Remove from the oven and raise the temperature to broil. Place about 4 inches from the flame, and broil until golden, 1 to 2 minutes.

NOTE: For cracked black pepper, wrap peppercorns in a dish towel and smash them with a heavy pan.

Wish Macaroni and Cheese

The great Italian flavors in this creamy dish (from the chef of South Beach's popular Wish restaurant) come from savory pancetta, Parmigiano-Reggiano, and buttery fontina.

10 tablespoons butter, plus extra for the baking dishes	1½ cups (6 ounces) grated Parmigiano-Reggiano cheese
1½ cups (almost ⅔ pound) small-diced pancetta	2½ cups (10 ounces) small-diced fontina cheese, cold
½ dry baguette	Kosher salt
1 pound rotelle	Freshly ground pepper
4 cups heavy cream	

1. Preheat the oven to 375°F. Lightly butter six individual baking dishes or a 9 by 13-inch baking pan.

2. Place the pancetta on a baking sheet and bake until just crisp, about 18 minutes. Drain off the fat and reserve the pancetta.

3. Crush the baguette into semifine crumbs (there will be about 1 cup; you may use a food processor). In a large sauté pan over medium heat, melt the 10 tablespoons of butter and toast the crumbs, tossing, until golden brown, 8 to 10 minutes. Set aside.

4. Bring a large pot of salted water to a boil over high heat and cook the macaroni until al dente, 8 to 10 minutes. Drain and place in a large mixing bowl.

5. In a large (4 quarts or more) saucepan over high heat, bring the heavy cream to a boil; lower the heat to medium and simmer until reduced by one third. It will still be pourable and thin. Slowly

whisk in 1¼ cups of the Parmigiano-Reggiano and all the pancetta, and continue reducing until thick.

6. Add the cream mixture and the fontina to the macaroni in the bowl and toss quickly to mix. Season with salt and pepper. Pour the mixture into the prepared baking dishes or large pan and top with the bread crumbs and remaining ¼ cup of Parmigiano-Reggiano. Bake until bubbling and golden, 12 to 15 minutes for the small dishes or 15 to 20 minutes for the large pan.

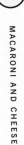

Mozzarella Mac

MAKES 6 TO 8 SERVINGS

Although the ingredients may bring to mind images of pizza, this is a surprisingly fresh and delicate Mac. The best-quality mozzarella and ripe tomatoes—beefsteak or plum—are key. After a short stay in the oven, the creamy mozzarella sauce infuses the pasta, the tomatoes are barely softened, and the basil ribbons remain bright green and flavorful.

1 pound rigatoni or penne rigate	Kosher salt
Butter for the baking dish	Freshly ground pepper
2 cups half-and-half	2 medium beefsteak tomatoes or 4 large plum tomatoes, juice and seeds squeezed out, cut into medium dice
½ pound mozzarella cheese, cut into small dice (2 cups)	
2 cups plus 2 tablespoons (just over ½ pound) grated Parmigiano-Reggiano cheese	15 basil leaves, cut into thin ribbons

53

1. Bring a large pot of salted water to a boil over high heat and cook the pasta until al dente, 8 to 10 minutes. Drain and place in a large mixing bowl.

2. Preheat the oven to 375°F. Butter a 9 by 13-inch baking dish.

3. In a medium saucepan over medium-high heat, combine the cream, the mozzarella, and 2 cups of the Parmigiano-Reggiano and bring to a simmer. Reduce the heat to medium and cook, stirring frequently, until the mozzarella has melted and the sauce is slightly thickened. Taste and season with salt (carefully—the Parmigiano-Reggiano may be salty) and pepper. Remove from the heat and stir in the tomatoes and basil. Pour the mixture over the pasta and mix thoroughly.

4. Pour into the prepared dish and sprinkle with the remaining 2 tablespoons of grated Parmigiano-Reggiano. Bake until heated through, 15 to 20 minutes. Allow to sit for 5 minutes before serving.

Macaroni Gratin Mas Antoine

MAKES 6 TO 8 SERVINGS

It's hard to stop eating this gratin from the chef-owner of Bouterin restaurant in Manhattan; his mother, herself a talented cook, prepared this treat in the kitchen of the family's farm in Saint-Rémy-de-Provence. Wild thyme grew just outside the farmhouse (which was called Mas Antoine), along with lavender and other fragrant herbs.

2 tablespoons butter, plus extra for the gratin dish	6 drops of Tabasco or pinch of cayenne pepper
1 pound elbow macaroni	1 teaspoon minced fresh thyme
2 generous tablespoons flour	Pinch of freshly grated nutmeg
2 1/2 cups whole milk	2 cups (1/2 pound) grated Swiss cheese
Generous pinch of kosher salt	3 tablespoons seasoned bread crumbs

1. Preheat the oven to 400°F. Butter a 9 by 13-inch gratin dish or baking pan.

2. Bring a large pot of salted water to a boil over high heat and cook the pasta until al dente, 8 to 10 minutes. Drain and place in a large bowl.

3. In a large saucepan over medium-high heat, melt the 2 tablespoons of butter. Sprinkle the flour over it and mix well with a spatula or wooden spoon; cook about 2 minutes. Raise the heat to high, slowly whisk in the milk, and bring to a boil, whisking. Add the salt, Tabasco, thyme, nutmeg, and cheese and mix well. Lower the heat to medium and cook, stirring, until the cheese is almost com-

pletely melted and the mixture is thick. Pour the sauce over the macaroni, mix well, and pour into the buttered dish. Sprinkle with the bread crumbs.

4. Bake on the middle shelf until brown and firm, 25 to 30 minutes. If the top has not browned, place under a preheated broiler just until brown and crisp.

Macaroni and Cheese Provençal with Cod

MAKES 4 TO 6 SERVINGS

The cod is savory and the veggies are crunchy-perfect in this enticing combination of flavors and textures created by the founder and chef of Boston's Hamersley's Bistro. Serve this Mediterranean-inspired dish with a generous ladle, to make sure you get plenty of the delicious sauce.

½ pound penne

½ pound salt cod, soaked and drained (soak for 8 to 24 hours in four changes of cold water, until it feels fresh and tastes barely salty)

4 tablespoons olive oil, plus extra for the baking dish and drizzling

1 medium head fennel (just over 1 pound), cut into medium dice

1 small onion, cut into small dice

5 cloves garlic, finely chopped

1 tablespoon flour

1 red bell pepper, seeded and cut into medium dice

2 cups blanched, peeled, seeded, and chopped fresh tomatoes (4 medium tomatoes), or substitute canned

1 cup white wine

¼ cup (1 ounce) coarsely grated sharp Cheddar cheese

½ cup (4 ounces) pitted and coarsely chopped black calamata olives

1 cup firmly packed shredded basil leaves

Kosher salt

Freshly ground pepper

¼ cup (1 ounce) coarsely grated Asiago cheese

2 tablespoons grated Parmesan cheese

2 tablespoons grated Pecorino Romano cheese

1 shallot, sliced very thin and separated into rings

¼ cup fresh bread crumbs

1. Preheat the oven to 350°F.
2. Bring a large pot of salted water to a boil over high heat and cook the pasta until al dente, 10 to 12 minutes. Drain.

3. Place a pot large enough to hold the cod over high heat and bring 1 quart of water to a boil. Add the cod, lower the heat to medium, and simmer for 10 to 12 minutes. Drain in a colander, reserving 1 cup of the cod liquid. Remove any bones, skin, or fat and flake the cod into bite-size pieces.

4. Heat the 4 tablespoons of olive oil in a large saucepan over medium heat. Add the fennel, onion, garlic, and flour and cook for 2 minutes, stirring occasionally. Add the bell pepper, tomatoes, and wine and continue cooking until the vegetables are cooked through, about 20 minutes. Add the Cheddar and stir until melted. Add the cod, olives, and basil and stir to combine. Stir in some of the reserved cooking water if the mixture seems a bit dry (this will depend upon how much juice the tomatoes release). Season with salt and pepper and remove from the heat.

5. Mix the pasta and the salt cod mixture together so the sauce coats the pasta evenly. Pour into a lightly oiled 9 by 13-inch baking dish.

6. Mix the remaining cheeses with the sliced shallot and bread crumbs. Sprinkle the cheese mixture evenly on top of the pasta. Drizzle with additional olive oil, if desired. Bake on the middle shelf until the pasta is bubbling and the top is crisp and browned, 25 to 30 minutes.

Greek (and Organic) Macaroni and Cheese

MAKES 4 TO 6 SERVINGS

An amazing dish with lively colors and textures, this suggests a Greek salad transformed. Chef Pouillon of Nora and Asia Nora, in Washington, D.C., uses only organic ingredients here and in all the food she cooks, and they are worth seeking out when you shop. Feta contrasts with the sweet, juicy tomatoes and fresh spinach, and the herbs sing of Greece.

1 pound macaroni	2 teaspoons minced fresh thyme
1/2 pound spinach, washed and stemmed	1 tablespoon finely chopped garlic
1 1/2 pounds crumbled feta cheese (about 6 cups)	1/2 teaspoon red pepper flakes, or to taste
2 1/3 cups whole milk	1/2 cup pitted and coarsely chopped black olives, optional
2 tablespoons fresh lemon juice	1/2 pound cherry tomatoes, halved
2/3 cup olive oil	1/2 cup grated Parmesan cheese
1 teaspoon kosher salt	1/4 cup mixed chopped fresh herbs, such as parsley, thyme, and rosemary
2 teaspoons freshly ground pepper	
3/4 teaspoon minced fresh rosemary	

1. Preheat the oven to 350°F.
2. Bring 6 quarts of salted water to a boil. Add the pasta and cook, stirring occasionally, until al dente, 8 to 10 minutes. Drain and place in a large mixing bowl.

3. Blanch the spinach: Bring 4 quarts of salted water to a simmer over medium-high heat. Have ready a large bowl of ice water and a slotted spoon. Add the spinach to the simmering water (in three or four batches) and submerge it. Let it cook for about 15 seconds, remove with the slotted spoon, and plunge into the ice water. Let the spinach cool completely, drain it, and squeeze out the excess water. If the leaves are large, chop them into bite-size pieces. Reserve.

4. In a blender or food processor, puree the feta cheese with the milk, lemon juice, olive oil, salt, and pepper. Blend in two batches, if necessary. This will not be completely smooth; there will be very small chunks of cheese remaining. Stir the cheese mixture into the cooked pasta, then add the minced rosemary and thyme, the garlic, red pepper flakes, olives, cherry tomatoes, and blanched spinach.

5. Place in a 9 by 13-inch baking pan and sprinkle with the grated Parmesan cheese and the mixed herbs. Bake on the middle shelf until the pasta is heated through and the top is slightly browned, 25 to 30 minutes.

Pastitsio

The vibrant flavors and textures in this hearty Greek classic from the chef of New York's Molyvos restaurant will bring you back for seconds and thirds. When you set this out on your buffet table, it will disappear in a flash.

Pastitsio is a complex dish with many enticing ingredients in addition to pasta and cheese, so be sure to leave a few hours for preparation. It helps to make the components ahead and refrigerate them separately; you can also complete the dish a day in advance and reheat it before serving. But this one is well worth your time—Pastitsio will make your party.

FOR THE FILLING

1/4 cup currants

9 tablespoons olive oil

1 pound ground beef (90% lean)

1 pound ground lamb, or substitute another pound of beef

Kosher salt

Freshly ground pepper

3 1/2 tablespoons *ras el hanout* (see Note and Sources)

2 teaspoons ground Aleppo pepper (see Note and Sources)

2 1/2 tablespoons ground cinnamon

4 cups finely diced onion (2 large onions, about 1 1/2 pounds)

6 cloves garlic, thinly sliced

2 cups red wine

2 1/2 cups canned whole tomatoes (from a 28-ounce can; keep any extra for another use), crushed by hand, with their juice

1. In a small bowl, cover the currants with warm water and let soak for 30 minutes. Drain and reserve.

2. Heat a large skillet or a 4- to 6-quart pot over medium heat until hot. Add 2 tablespoons of the olive

oil, swirl to coat the pan, and add one quarter of the beef and lamb in small bits. Cook, stirring to break up the meat, until lightly browned. Season with a generous pinch of salt and pepper, $1/4$ teaspoon each of *ras el hanout* and Aleppo pepper, and a pinch of cinnamon. Remove from the heat and, with a slotted spatula or spoon, transfer the meat to a bowl. Pour off any excess oil and wipe out the pan with a paper towel; repeat the process until all the meat has been cooked.

3. Return the skillet to the stove over medium heat and heat the remaining tablespoon of olive oil until shimmering. Add the onions and cook until translucent, about 5 minutes. Add the garlic and cook another minute, stirring once to combine. Return the meat to the pan and season with the remaining *ras el hanout,* Aleppo pepper, and cinnamon. Stir to combine well (be careful—the pan will be quite full). Add the wine and reduce the liquid until the mixture is almost dry, 35 to 40 minutes. Stir it occasionally, since the bottom will be drier than the top. Add the tomatoes with their juices, reduce the heat to low, and cook for 5 minutes, stirring once to combine. Add the currants, taste, and adjust the seasoning with salt and pepper. Cook for another 5 minutes. Remove the pan from the heat and transfer the meat to a large bowl to cool.

4. May be refrigerated for up to one day.

FOR THE TOMATO SAUCE

$1/4$ cup olive oil

4 cloves garlic, thinly sliced

1 teaspoon dried Greek oregano

Kosher salt

Freshly ground pepper

1 28-ounce can crushed tomatoes, with juice

In a medium saucepan over medium heat, heat the oil until shimmering and sauté the garlic for 2 to 3 minutes. Add the oregano and season with salt and pepper. Sauté for 1 minute more, add the crushed tomatoes, stir once to combine (most of the oil will float to the top), and bring to a boil. Reduce the heat to low and simmer for 25 minutes, stirring occasionally and skimming the surface if necessary. Can be refrigerated, covered, for up to five days, or frozen.

FOR THE YOGURT-BÉCHAMEL TOPPING	Scant ½ cup flour
1½ cups whole milk	Kosher salt
1½ cups heavy cream	Freshly ground pepper
1 bay leaf	Freshly grated nutmeg
½ medium onion	½ cup goat's milk yogurt (available at specialty and health food stores and some greenmarkets)
2 whole cloves	or cow's milk yogurt, drained in a cheesecloth-lined strainer until thick
2 tablespoons butter, softened	

1. Combine the milk and cream in a large, heavy pot, place over medium heat, and bring the milk mixture to a simmer.

2. Meanwhile, lay the bay leaf over the cut side of the onion and pierce it with the cloves; the bay leaf will adhere. Set aside.

3. In a large pot over medium heat, melt the butter and stir in the flour. Blend until smooth and thick (the mixture will resemble thick mashed potatoes). Cook the mixture over low heat for 10 minutes; remove from the heat and whisk in the milk mixture in a steady stream. Place the pot over medium heat, add the clove-studded onion, and cook for 10 minutes, whisking occasionally to make it smooth. Season with salt, pepper, and nutmeg and set aside to cool.

4. When the béchamel comes to room temperature, remove the onion, fold in the yogurt, and combine well. If it isn't smooth, whisk again.

FOR THE PASTA
1 pound penne

2 tablespoons olive oil

Bring a large pot of salted water to a boil over high heat and cook the pasta until al dente (approximately 12 minutes), stirring occasionally to keep it moving freely in the water. Drain in a colander and transfer to a pot of cold water with ice, to stop the cooking process. When the pasta has cooled, drain well and place in a mixing bowl. Toss with the olive oil, to keep it from sticking.

TO ASSEMBLE

**¹/₄ cup (about 1 ounce) grated kefalotyri cheese,
or substitute grated Parmesan cheese**

1. Preheat the oven to 450°F.

2. Spread ³/₄ cup of the tomato sauce in a 9 by 13 by 4-inch baking dish (or use two smaller, shallower baking dishes), covering the bottom thoroughly. Add ¹/₄ to ¹/₂ cup of the tomato sauce to the reserved penne and toss to coat. Spread the pasta evenly in the baking dish and spread the meat mixture over the pasta. Pour the yogurt mixture over the meat and sprinkle with the kefalotyri cheese.

3. Put the baking dish on a sheet pan and bake on the middle shelf for 25 minutes. Turn the oven setting to broil and finish the Pastitsio under the broiler until browned, 3 to 5 minutes. Serve hot (use a slotted spoon).

N O T E : *Ras el hanout* (literally "head of the shop"), a Middle Eastern spice blend, contains cinnamon, nutmeg, cloves, turmeric, ginger, and cardamom, among other flavors. Aleppo pepper is made from dried, lightly salted Turkish chiles.

Macaroni and Feta Salad

MAKES 4 TO 6 SERVINGS

Here, again, are the appealing flavors and textures of a tangy, fresh Greek salad. Macaroni is the mellowing influence, and it fits right in.

½ pound elbow macaroni	1 small red onion, thinly sliced and slices halved
7 tablespoons olive oil	12 black Greek olives, pitted and halved
2 tablespoons fresh lemon juice or white wine vinegar	10 small radishes, thinly sliced
1 teaspoon dried Greek oregano	½ pound cherry tomatoes, halved
Kosher salt	1 cup (¼ pound) crumbled feta cheese
Freshly ground pepper	2 tablespoons minced flat-leaf parsley

1. Bring a large pot of salted water to a boil over high heat and cook the pasta until al dente, 8 to 10 minutes. Drain, place in a large salad bowl, and toss with 1 tablespoon of the olive oil. Let cool to room temperature.

2. For the dressing, combine the lemon juice with the oregano and a pinch of salt and pepper, and whisk in the remaining 6 tablespoons of olive oil.

3. Add the onion, olives, radishes, tomatoes, and feta to the macaroni and toss to combine. Add the dressing, season with salt and pepper, and toss again to combine. Stir in the parsley.

Macaroni and Manchego

A stovetop version, this is easy to make and subtly flavored, and with its fresh, herbal notes, it is perfect for warmer weather (as we would expect from Chef Allen's restaurant in Miami). Chef Allen tells us that Manchego is one of Spain's most popular cheeses, whose simplicity makes for a comfortable combination with the fennel and macaroni.

3 tablespoons kosher salt	2 tablespoons butter, at room temperature
1 pound elbow macaroni	1 cup (1/4 pound) grated Manchego cheese
2 tablespoons olive oil	2 tablespoons chopped fresh basil
3 large shallots, julienned (about 1/3 pound)	2 tablespoons chopped flat-leaf parsley
1 small fennel bulb, julienned (2/3 to 3/4 pound)	1/2 teaspoon red pepper flakes
1/2 teaspoon minced garlic	

1. In a deep pot, bring to a boil 4 quarts of water with 2 tablespoons of the salt. Add the macaroni and cook until al dente, 8 to 10 minutes. Drain.

2. In a 4-quart pot over medium heat, warm the olive oil and cook the shallots and fennel until softened and aromatic, 8 to 10 minutes. Add the garlic and cook for another minute.

3. Pour the hot macaroni into the shallot mixture. Return to medium heat and add the butter and Manchego cheese, mixing well until melted. Stir in the remaining salt, and the basil, parsley, and red pepper flakes. Transfer to a bowl and serve immediately.

Swiss Mac with Potatoes

The Swiss give us a simply prepared, basic Mac and Cheese that is eggy and hearty, with the added texture of potatoes. It will warm you up after a snowy day on the slopes.

Butter for the baking pan	2 cups (1/2 pound) coarsely grated Swiss cheese
1/2 pound elbow macaroni	3 eggs, lightly beaten
1 medium potato, peeled and sliced 1/2 inch thick, with slices cut into 11/2-inch strips	2 cups whole milk
Kosher salt	Freshly ground pepper

1. Preheat the oven to 350°F. Butter a 9 by 13-inch baking pan.

2. Bring a large pot of salted water to a boil over high heat and cook the pasta until al dente, 8 to 10 minutes. Drain.

3. Place the potato strips in a medium pot and cover with cold water by 1/2 inch. Add 1 tablespoon salt. Place over high heat, bring to a boil, and cook until the potatoes are softened but still firm, 8 to 9 minutes. Drain.

4. Layer the macaroni, potatoes, and cheese in the baking pan, ending with a layer of cheese (there should be two full layers of each ingredient). In a small bowl, mix the eggs, milk, salt, and pepper, and pour over the macaroni and potatoes. Bake on the middle shelf until hot and bubbly, 20 to 25 minutes.

Sweet Noodle and Cheese Kugel

MAKES 4 TO 8 SERVINGS

A family favorite, this makes a pleasing vanilla-scented luncheon entrée or a satisfying dessert—not to mention an outstanding nosh at any hour. Since noodle puddings can be quite heavy, I prefer to divide the mixture between two pans and get a lighter, thinner result.

Butter for the baking pans	1 cup whole milk
$^3/_4$ pound medium egg noodles	1 heaping teaspoon kosher salt
4 eggs, lightly beaten	$^3/_4$ cup plus 2 tablespoons sugar
$^1/_2$ pound (1 cup) cottage cheese	2 teaspoons vanilla
$^1/_2$ pound cream cheese, cut into small bits	$^1/_2$ cup dark raisins, optional
1 cup sour cream	2 teaspoons ground cinnamon

1. Preheat the oven to 350°F. Lightly butter two 8 by 8-inch baking pans.

2. Bring a large pot of salted water to a boil over high heat and cook the noodles, stirring occasionally, until al dente, about 8 minutes. Drain.

3. Meanwhile, in a large mixing bowl, combine the eggs, cheeses, sour cream, milk, salt, $^3/_4$ cup of the sugar, the vanilla, and raisins, if desired. Mix well with a wooden spoon or whisk (lumps of both cheeses will remain). Add the noodles and mix until combined. Divide the mixture between the prepared baking pans.

4. In a small bowl or cup, combine the remaining 2 tablespoons of sugar with the cinnamon and sprinkle evenly over the noodles. Bake until firm, 35 to 40 minutes.

PART 4

Mac and Cheese Today

alk about evolution! This section demonstrates how far our homespun dish has come, as skilled chefs with soaring imaginations deconstruct Mac and Cheese in ways both subtle and stunning. Wild mushrooms, chiles, salsa, fresh figs, dried cherries—even truffles and foie gras—now seem destined to meld with the classic dish and transform it.

Trying to organize the "Mac and Cheese Today" recipes by ingredients was no easy task. Just when I thought I had found a mushroom Mac or two, I discovered duck prosciutto and mascarpone, or artichoke hearts and prosciutto, in the same casserole. But there is a loose sort of progression, and here is a basic rundown:

Waldy Malouf's Penne with Roquefort creates a brand-new dish through an imaginative shift in cheeses; and Rocco DiSpirito's playful method recasts traditional ingredients into a novel, fun form in Macaroni and Cheese Croquettes.

Debra Ponzek's Farfalle with Fontina, Tasso Ham, and Baby Spinach displays the subtlety and perfect balance of components for which her recipes are known. Charlie Palmer uses luxurious but available ingredients in his sophisticated Macaroni with Cantal Cheese and Westphalian Ham.

Gordon Hamersley combines tradition and innovation in Macaroni and Cheese with Oysters and Pork Sausage and provides us with a visual (as well as culinary) treat in his beautiful Terrine of Macaroni, Goat Cheese, and Foie Gras.

The spicy kick of chiles electrifies contemporary Macs. Try Today's Macaroni and Cheese, from Rick Bayless; Macaroni with Many Cheeses in a Red Chile–Herb Crust, from Katy Sparks;

Steven Picker's Green Chile Mac and Cheese; and Scott Campbell's Mac and Smoked Cheddar with Ham and Chipotles.

Jeffrey Bank and Chris Metz, in Artie's Deli Mac and Cheese, add a really surprising flavor, one that unites Mac and Cheese with traditional deli fare: spicy pastrami. Who knew?

Kevin Johnson showcases wild mushrooms in Baked Macaroni with White Cheddar Cheese and Cremini Mushrooms. Mushrooms share the billing with savory accents in Janos Wilder's Macaroni with Duck Prosciutto, Chanterelles, and Mascarpone; as they do in Loren Falsone and Eric Moshier's Baked Cellentani with Four Cheeses, Prosciutto, Artichoke Hearts, and Portobellos. In Jody Adams's Baked Stuffed Pasta Spirals, their earthy note is enhanced by fresh figs and walnuts.

The flavor of truffles combined with macaroni and cheese presents a spectacular union of haute and homey, as offered by Andrew Carmellini, Fontina and White Truffle Macaroni; Mark Franz, Pasta with Fonduta and Fresh Truffles; David Burke, ONEc.p.s. Wild Mushroom and Truffle Macaroni and Cheese; Bobby Flay, Baked Conchiglie with Roasted Garlic–Cheese Sauce, Ricotta Cheese, and White Truffle Oil; and Tim Goodell, California Truffled Macaroni and Cheese. (Why hadn't we thought of these incredible combinations before?)

Alex Porter's seductively named Chunks of Lobster Swimming in Cheesy Macaroni is pure luxury; and Joseph Wrede's Joseph's Table Mac and Cheese with Dried Cherry Chutney and Roquefort Sauce is inspired whimsy.

And for dessert, Loren Falsone and Eric Moshier's ethereal Sweetened Mascarpone and Noodle Pudding gives you a whispered hint of noodle puddings past.

Penne with Roquefort

MAKES 6 TO 8 SERVINGS AS A MAIN DISH, 12 AS A SIDE DISH

Macaroni and cheese becomes a different dish entirely when the cheese is a bold, complex Roquefort. For anyone who loves Roquefort, this is pure bliss, courtesy of Waldy Malouf of New York's and Stamford's Beacon restaurants.

6 tablespoons butter, plus extra for the pan	1 teaspoon freshly ground pepper
1 pound penne	1 teaspoon freshly grated nutmeg
3 cups whole milk	4 cups (1 to 1¼ pounds) crumbled Roquefort cheese
6 tablespoons flour	½ cup (2 ounces) grated Parmesan cheese
2 teaspoons kosher salt	

1. Preheat the oven to 350°F. Butter a 9 by 13-inch pan or a 2- to 2½-quart baking dish or casserole.

2. Bring a large pot of salted water to a boil over high heat and cook the penne until al dente, 10 to 12 minutes. Drain and place in a large mixing bowl.

3. In a small saucepan over medium-high heat, bring the milk to a scald.

4. In a large, heavy saucepan over medium heat, melt the 6 tablespoons of butter. Add the flour and cook, stirring, 3 minutes. Stir in the heated milk and continue stirring until the sauce has thickened (3 to 5 minutes). Reduce the heat to low, add the salt, pepper, and nutmeg, and simmer for 4 to 5 minutes to meld the flavors.

5. Add the Roquefort and sauce to the penne and combine well. Pour the mixture into the baking pan and sprinkle with the grated Parmesan. Bake until the top is nicely browned and the sauce is bubbly, about 25 minutes.

Macaroni and Cheese Croquettes

MAKES 8 SERVINGS

Here is an ingenious new take on macaroni and cheese from the chef of Union Pacific, known for his skill and creativity. These savory, awesomely crisp, cheese-loaded croquettes are a kid's dream come true.

1 pound elbow macaroni	1/4 cup mayonnaise
2 cups (1/2 pound) coarsely grated sharp Cheddar cheese	1/2 teaspoon chopped flat-leaf parsley
1 cup (1/4 pound) coarsely grated Gruyère cheese	1 to 1 1/2 cups flour
Kosher salt	5 eggs, lightly beaten
Freshly ground pepper	1 cup plain or seasoned bread crumbs
1/4 cup sour cream	Canola oil for deep-frying

1. Bring a large pot of salted water to a boil over high heat and cook the pasta until al dente, 8 to 10 minutes. Drain and place in a mixing bowl. Add the Cheddar and Gruyère and mix well. Season with salt and pepper and set aside to cool.

2. When the mixture has cooled to room temperature, add the sour cream, mayonnaise, and parsley, mix well, and form into 8 large or 16 small balls. Dip each ball into flour to coat, dip into the beaten egg, and roll in the bread crumbs until well coated. (After each dip, resqueeze the balls back into shape.)

3. In a heavy pan, heat about 3 inches of canola oil to 365°F. Lower the balls into the oil with a slotted spoon and fry until browned on all sides (avoid crowding). If the oil starts to get white and foamy on top, discard and replace with fresh oil. Drain the croquettes on paper towels and serve hot.

Farfalle with Fontina, Tasso Ham, and Baby Spinach

Chef Ponzek's subtle Mediterranean touch defines this bright dish (from her two Aux Délices shops in Greenwich, Connecticut). It has superb flavor, just the right amount of cheesiness, the kick of savory ham, and the fresh note of baby spinach. There is no béchamel and preparation is quick and easy—put a pot of water on the fire and prepare your sauce while the pasta cooks.

1 pound farfalle or penne	1½ cups firmly packed, coarsely chopped baby spinach
1 tablespoon olive oil	½ pound tasso ham or Black Forest ham, cut into ¼-inch dice
2 shallots, finely diced (about 2 tablespoons)	Kosher salt
2 cups heavy cream	Freshly ground pepper
2 cups (½ pound) grated fontina cheese	

1. Bring 6 quarts of salted water to a boil. Add the pasta and cook, stirring occasionally, until al dente, 9 to 10 minutes. Drain and reserve.

2. Preheat the broiler. Set out six individual heatproof bowls or a larger heatproof serving bowl.

3. Meanwhile, in a large saucepan, heat the olive oil over medium-high heat until almost smoking. Add the shallots and sauté until translucent (this will take only about a minute). Add the cream and bring to a boil; stir, and reduce until slightly thickened, 3 to 4 minutes. Add the cheese and stir until

smooth. The sauce will be thick. Stir in the spinach and ham and remove from the heat. Add the cooked pasta and toss until lightly coated. Season with salt and pepper.

4. Divide among the smaller bowls or pour into the serving bowl. Place under the broiler until golden brown, 2 to 3 minutes.

Macaroni with Cantal Cheese and Westphalian Ham

The finest ingredients will indeed give you the finest dish. Cantal cheese from France lends a smooth, refined flavor, and Westphalian ham, cured and then slowly smoked, adds a light, savory touch. Chef Palmer (with well-known restaurants in New York City, Los Angeles, Las Vegas, and Sonoma, California) refines technique as well, lightening the macaroni and cheese mixture with beaten egg whites, as for a soufflé. This is a transcendent—but never fussy—Mac.

Butter for the casserole

1 pound elbow macaroni, orecchiette, mini rigatoni, or other short, tubular pasta

1½ cups heavy cream

2 tablespoons canola oil

2 cups diced onion

1 tablespoon roasted garlic puree (see Note)

2 tablespoons Wondra flour

¼ cup dry white wine

1½ cups (about 6 ounces) finely chopped Cantal cheese

2 cups (about ½ pound) finely diced Westphalian ham

1 tablespoon minced flat-leaf parsley

Tabasco, to taste

Kosher salt

Freshly ground white pepper

3 egg whites

¾ cup bread crumbs

1. Preheat the oven to 350°F. Generously butter a 2-quart casserole.

2. Bring 6 quarts of salted water to a boil. Add the pasta and cook, stirring occasionally, until al dente, 9 to 10 minutes. Drain and reserve.

3. Heat the cream in a small saucepan over medium heat.

4. Heat the oil in a large nonstick skillet over medium heat, and sauté the onion until nicely browned and slightly crisp, about 15 minutes. Stir in the garlic puree. Reduce the heat to medium-low and stir in the flour until incorporated into the oil and pan juices. Raise the heat to medium; whisk in the hot cream and then the wine. Cook, stirring constantly, until the mixture has begun to thicken.

5. Turn off the heat and stir in the cheese. When the cheese has melted, mix in the ham and half the parsley. Add the drained pasta and stir to combine. Season to taste with Tabasco, salt, and pepper.

6. Beat the egg whites until they hold soft peaks and gently fold them into the pasta mixture until just barely blended. Pour the mixture into the prepared casserole.

7. Combine the bread crumbs with the remaining parsley and sprinkle over the casserole. Bake until the bread crumbs are browned and the edges are bubbling, about 30 minutes. Serve hot.

NOTE: To roast the garlic, preheat the oven to 300°F. Cut off the bud end and rub the head of garlic with olive oil. Wrap loosely in foil, place on a baking pan, and roast until very soft, 45 minutes to 1 hour. Peel, or squeeze out the softened garlic, and mash (can be refrigerated up to one day).

Macaroni and Cheese with Oysters and Pork Sausage

MAKES 4 SERVINGS

Oysters and macaroni are classic New England partners. In his exciting recipe, Chef Hamersley brings the combination into the twenty-first century and adds new layers of flavor, spice, and texture.

½ pound penne	½ cup (2 ounces) coarsely grated Asiago cheese
3 tablespoons butter, plus extra for the baking dish	Kosher salt
1 small onion (about ¼ pound), cut into small dice	Freshly ground pepper
¼ teaspoon herbes de Provence	½ pound sausage meat
2 tablespoons flour	1 to 2 tablespoons Tabasco, or to taste, optional
1 cup whole milk	16 medium oysters, shucked, excess liquid drained
1 cup light cream	1 shallot, sliced very thin and separated into rings
2 cups (½ pound) coarsely grated Gruyère cheese	½ cup fresh bread crumbs
½ cup (2 ounces) coarsely grated sharp white Cheddar cheese, preferably Vermont	

1. Bring a large pot of salted water to a boil over high heat and cook the pasta until al dente, 10 to 12 minutes. Drain.

2. Preheat the oven to 350°F. Butter an 8 by 8-inch (2-quart) baking dish.

3. In a large saucepan over medium heat, melt the 3 tablespoons of butter. Add the onion and herbes

de Provence and cook until the onion has softened, 5 to 6 minutes. Add the flour and cook an additional 8 minutes, stirring occasionally; it will become golden brown. Do not allow the mixture to burn.

4. Reduce the heat to medium-low, whisk in the milk and cream, and cook for 5 minutes, stirring occasionally. Add 1 1/2 cups of the Gruyère, 1/4 cup of the Cheddar, and 1/4 cup of the Asiago. Cook slowly, stirring occasionally, until the cheeses are melted and incorporated into the sauce; season with salt and pepper. The sauce will be very thick. Remove from the heat and set aside.

5. In a small sauté pan over medium heat, cook the sausage meat for 10 minutes. Drain off the fat, and add the Tabasco, if desired (with care—Tabasco is very assertive).

6. Add the pasta, sausage, and oysters to the cheese sauce, mixing well so the sauce coats the pasta evenly. Pour the mixture into the prepared baking dish.

7. Mix the remaining cheese with the sliced shallot and the bread crumbs, and sprinkle evenly over the pasta. Bake on the middle shelf until the pasta is bubbling and the top is crisp and brown, about 30 minutes.

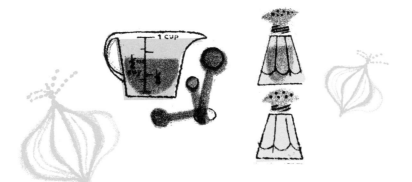

Terrine of Macaroni, Goat Cheese, and Foie Gras

MAKES 4 TO 6 SERVINGS

Chef Hamersley's terrine will be the star of your table, with its eye-catching colors and layers of glorious ingredients. It requires careful preparation, but it can be made a day in advance, refrigerated, and then served at room temperature.

1 10-ounce bag fresh spinach, washed and stemmed, to line the mold

1/2 pound penne or ziti

1/2 pound raw foie gras, duck pâté, or cooked foie gras product

Kosher salt

Freshly ground pepper

3 tablespoons vegetable oil

1/2 cup Armagnac (or substitute Cognac)

1 medium red onion, diced (about 1 cup)

3 leeks, white part and a bit of tender green, trimmed, washed, and diced (about 3 1/2 cups)

2 tablespoons chopped fresh thyme

2 cups duck stock (available frozen at gourmet or specialty stores), or substitute chicken stock or canned low-sodium chicken broth

2 envelopes unflavored gelatin

1 1/2 to 2 cups (1/3 to 1/2 pound) crumbled goat cheese

1. Bring a large pot of salted water to a boil and blanch the spinach until still bright green, about 5 seconds. Remove and place in a bowl of ice water. Once it is cold, drain and pat out some of the liquid. Do not squeeze, or the leaves will lose their shape.

2. Line a 1 1/2-quart mold with plastic wrap, leaving a 4-inch overhang on all sides. Line the mold with the blanched spinach leaves: use the big leaves first and place them shiny side down and vein side

up on the bottom and up the sides, leaving about a $1/2$-inch overhang. Try to keep the lining one layer thick, but you may patch any holes or tears with the smaller leaves. Reserve any remaining spinach leaves for the top.

3. Bring a large pot of salted water to a boil over high heat and cook the pasta until al dente, 8 to 10 minutes. Drain and reserve.

4. Rinse the foie gras and pat dry. Using a small sharp knife, trim away large veins and membranes. Slice approximately $3/4$ inch thick. Season the slices lightly with salt and pepper.

5. In a sauté pan over medium-high heat, heat 1 tablespoon of the oil until hot, add the uncooked foie gras slices, and sear for 15 to 20 seconds on each side; be careful not to overcook and melt the foie gras. Remove and reserve in a bowl. Pour the Armagnac into the pan and reduce by three fourths, scraping up all the bits of cooked foie gras from the bottom, about 10 minutes. Pour the reduced Armagnac over the foie gras slices. (If you use pâté or cooked foie gras, do not cook it. Place the slices in a bowl and pour the reduced Armagnac over them.)

6. In another sauté pan, heat the remaining 2 tablespoons of oil over medium heat until shimmering. Add the onion and leeks and cook, stirring occasionally, until tender, about 15 minutes. Stir in the thyme and remove from the heat. Season with salt and pepper.

7. In a small saucepan over medium heat, warm the duck stock; add the gelatin, and stir to dissolve. Keep warm over low heat.

8. Layer half the ingredients in the mold in this order: pasta, foie gras, onion-leek mixture, and goat cheese. Sprinkle with salt and pepper and a few spoonfuls of stock, pressing down with a spatula so the stock fills up the pasta tubes. Repeat with the remaining ingredients.

9. Fold the overhanging spinach leaves over the top, or cover with a layer of spinach leaves shiny side up, and wrap the whole terrine in plastic wrap. Place on a plate and weight with heavy cans. Refrigerate 8 to 12 hours.

10. Remove the plastic wrap, run the blade of a thin, flexible knife around the inside of the mold, and invert the terrine onto a platter. Cut the terrine into $1/2$-inch slices.

Today's Macaroni and Cheese

Rick Bayless, chef and owner of Chicago's Frontera Grill and Topolobampo, confesses that he grew up on the wonderful slow-baked macaroni and cheese served at his parents' restaurant, which he calls "crusty cheese over submissive macaroni." His adult version is creamy and a little "edgy"—with the delicious jolt of salsa.

2 cups milk

4 tablespoons butter

¼ cup flour

2 cups good-quality salsa (such as Rick Bayless's Frontera brand Roasted Jalapeño Tomato, or Roasted Poblano Tomato)

3 cups (¾ pound) shredded Cheddar cheese

Kosher salt, about 1½ teaspoons

1 pound dried pasta (elbow macaroni, cavatappi, rotini, or fusilli)

Chopped fresh cilantro, for garnish

1. Fill a large pot with about 6 quarts of water and set over high heat. Warm the milk in a small saucepan over medium heat, or in a glass measuring cup in a microwave, for about 1 minute. In a medium saucepan, melt the butter over medium heat, then stir in the flour and whisk until the mixture turns a deep golden, about 2 minutes. Add the warmed milk all at once and continue to whisk constantly until the mixture thickens and comes to a full boil, 4 or 5 minutes. (Whisk diligently and there will be no lumps.) Stir in the salsa, remove from the heat, then stir in the cheese, stirring until it melts. Taste and season generously with salt.

2. When the water has come to a boil, add the pasta. Stir well so no pieces stick together and boil until

the pasta is al dente, about 10 minutes. Drain thoroughly and return to the pot. Stir in the cheese sauce, then spoon into a serving dish. Sprinkle with the cilantro.

NOTE: If you want a wonderful contrasting texture, spoon the macaroni and cheese into a buttered baking dish. Top with $1/2$ cup bread crumbs mixed with 1 tablespoon melted butter and bake in a preheated 375°F oven for 10 to 12 minutes, until richly browned and crisp.

Macaroni with Many Cheeses in a Red Chile–Herb Crust

MAKES 4 TO 6 SERVINGS

This is ideal to put together when you find yourself with many small bundles of cheese scraps in your refrigerator, says Chef Sparks, of Quilty's restaurant in Manhattan. And she advises that the pasta should be the best brand available, made from semolina flour and of good, even color.

When you lift this out of the oven, the heady aroma of anchos invites you to dig in. Serve with a salad of baby greens, to refresh the palate.

10 thyme stems (leaves reserved to use in the red chile–herb crust)

2 teaspoons whole coriander seeds

1/2 teaspoon dried orange peel

1 bay leaf

6 tablespoons butter, plus extra for the gratin dish

2 shallots, minced (about 1/3 cup)

1 cup (about 1/4 pound) thinly sliced shiitake mushroom caps

3/4 cup dry white wine

3 cups heavy cream

1 cup panko (Japanese bread crumbs)

2 teaspoons ancho chile powder (not commercial chile powder)

1 teaspoon minced fresh tarragon

1 teaspoon minced fresh thyme leaves (reserve thyme stems)

2 teaspoons minced fresh parsley

Kosher salt

Freshly ground pepper

1 pound farfalle

12 ounces mixed cheeses, grated, shredded, or broken into small pieces (best choices: goat cheeses, Camembert, Brie, Parmesan, Cheddar, Gruyère; best to avoid: smoked cheeses, Limburger!)

Freshly grated nutmeg

1. Make an herb sachet: Place the thyme stems, coriander seeds, dried orange peel, and bay leaf on a small square of cheesecloth. Bring the ends of the cheesecloth together and tie with kitchen string.

2. Melt 2 tablespoons of the butter in a large saucepan over medium heat. Add the shallots and sweat until soft, about 3 minutes; add the shiitakes and cook 3 additional minutes. Add the wine and reduce until almost dry, about 20 minutes. Add the cream and the sachet and simmer, stirring occasionally, until the cream has reduced by half, about 30 minutes.

3. Remove the sachet. Remove the pot from the heat and cover loosely.

4. Make the red chile–herb crust: Melt the remaining 4 tablespoons of butter in a sauté pan over medium heat. Add the panko and stir occasionally until the crumbs become golden brown, about 5 minutes. Add the ancho powder, tarragon, thyme leaves, and parsley and stir until well incorporated. Remove from the heat and season lightly with salt and pepper.

5. Preheat the oven to 400°F. Lightly butter a 9 by 13-inch gratin dish.

6. Cook the farfalle in boiling salted water until just al dente, about 8 minutes, and drain. Off the heat, stir the pasta into the still-warm sauce and add the cheeses. Season to taste with freshly grated nutmeg, salt, and pepper. Pour the pasta mixture into the gratin dish and sprinkle the crust mixture evenly over the entire surface.

7. Bake on the middle shelf for about 10 minutes or until the sauce bubbles around the edges. Remove from the heat and let cool 3 to 5 minutes before serving.

Green Chile Mac and Cheese

From the chef of Good restaurant in New York, here is a great Mac for chile lovers. Poblanos, the peppers you often see as chiles rellenos, are hot and flavorful; they give the dish exactly the right amount of spice and an exciting southwestern touch. Tortilla crumbs add texture and ripe tomato makes the perfect garnish.

When charring the peppers, be sure to keep the area well ventilated—this can be a smoky job.

1 pound elbow macaroni

Butter for the gratin dishes

3 cups heavy cream

1 cup roasted poblano puree (see Notes)

¼ cup chopped fresh cilantro

2 teaspoons kosher salt

1 teaspoon freshly ground pepper

2 cups (½ pound) grated Monterey Jack cheese

¾ cup (3 ounces) grated Parmigiano-Reggiano cheese

3 cups medium corn tortilla crumbs (see Notes)

1 small ripe tomato, cut into small dice

Fresh cilantro sprigs, for garnish

1. Bring a large pot of salted water to a boil over high heat and cook the macaroni until al dente, 8 to 10 minutes. Drain.

2. Preheat the broiler. Lightly butter six individual gratin dishes or shallow ovenproof bowls or a 9 by 13-inch baking dish.

3. In a medium saucepan over medium heat, combine the cream, poblano puree, chopped cilantro, salt, and pepper and bring to a simmer, about 7 minutes; simmer 3 minutes more to meld the flavors. Stir in the macaroni and cook until the cream returns to a simmer, 3 to 5 minutes. Add the

grated cheeses and bring the mixture back to a simmer, stirring constantly until the cheeses are melted.

4. Divide the mixture among the gratin dishes or bowls or pour into the baking dish. Sprinkle with tortilla crumbs to cover completely, and gently flatten with a large spoon. Place under the broiler until the topping is golden brown, about 2 minutes (watch carefully so it doesn't burn). Garnish with diced tomato and cilantro sprigs.

NOTES:

FOR THE ROASTED POBLANO PUREE

6 or 7 poblano chiles (about 1¾ pounds)

1. Turn a stove burner to high, place the poblanos directly on it, and turn, using tongs, until charred on all sides, about 12 minutes. Place in a brown paper bag, and close the bag (making sure that there are no burning embers on the chiles), or in a bowl covered tightly with plastic wrap, until cool enough to handle. Then rub off the skin and remove the stems and seeds. Puree in a blender and reserve. There should be about 1 cup of puree.

2. A good place to peel the peppers is in the sink under running water. This makes it easy to rinse out extra seeds, as well.

FOR THE TORTILLA CRUMBS

About 14 tortilla chips

Pulse in the food processor to medium crumbs.

Mac and Smoked Cheddar with Ham and Chipotles

Here is Chef Campbell's (of New York's Avenue restaurant) spicy, upbeat version of an old favorite. It has a great smoky taste that is just zesty enough, plus delicious crusts on both the top and bottom. When you dip your serving spoon into the top, you can hear the crust crackle—a welcoming sound if ever there was one.

4 tablespoons butter, plus extra for the baking pan and topping

⅓ cup panko (Japanese bread crumbs)

¾ pound elbow macaroni

2½ cups whole milk

¼ cup flour

2½ cups (10 ounces) grated smoked Cheddar cheese

⅓ cup julienned smoked ham

4 chipotle peppers (smoked jalapeños), or to taste, stemmed, seeded, and julienned (see Note)

Kosher salt

Freshly ground pepper

½ cup (2 ounces) grated Parmesan cheese

1. Preheat the oven to 400°F. Butter the bottom of a 9 by 13-inch baking pan and sprinkle lightly with half the crumbs.

2. Bring a large pot of salted water to a boil. Add the pasta and cook, stirring occasionally, until al dente, 8 to 10 minutes. Drain well and transfer to a large bowl.

3. Warm the milk in a small saucepan over medium heat or in the microwave.

4.   In a large saucepan over medium-low heat, melt the 4 tablespoons of butter; when it starts to bubble, whisk in the flour. Cook, stirring occasionally, for 3 to 4 minutes and then whisk in the warm milk. Reduce the heat to low and cook, stirring continually, for 15 minutes. Add the Cheddar, ham, and chipotles and stir until the cheese is melted. The mixture will be somewhat thin. Season with salt and pepper. Pour the mixture over the macaroni and mix well.

5.   Pour the macaroni and sauce into the prepared pan. Sprinkle with the remaining bread crumbs and the Parmesan cheese and dot with butter. Bake on the middle shelf until bubbling and a rich golden-brown color, with the sides starting to turn brown, 25 to 30 minutes. Let rest for 10 to 15 minutes before serving.

NOTE: Some tips for cutting chipotles: Use a plastic (or other nonwood) work surface so the aroma and flavor don't carry over to other foods. If you have sensitive skin, wear gloves when working with the peppers and wash your hands with soap when you are done. Keep your fingers away from your eyes!

JEFFREY BANK AND CHRIS METZ

Artie's Deli Mac and Cheese

MAKES 4 TO 6 SERVINGS

Pastrami, the highly spiced cured and smoked beef, adds zing to a creamy Mac and Cheese, as well as a bit of true New York taste. This is an unusual combination—but an addictive one.

4 tablespoons butter, plus extra for the baking dish	2 tablespoons grated Parmesan cheese
1/2 pound farfalle	1/4 pound pastrami, diced (scant cup)
1/4 cup flour	1 teaspoon kosher salt
2 cups whole milk	1/8 teaspoon freshly ground pepper
2 cups (1/2 pound) grated sharp Cheddar cheese	6 to 10 Ritz crackers, pulsed in the food processor, about 1/4 to 1/3 cup crumbs

1. Preheat the oven to 350°F. Butter an 8 by 8-inch baking dish.

2. Bring a large pot of salted water to a boil over high heat and cook the farfalle until al dente, 8 to 10 minutes. Drain.

3. In a large saucepan over medium-low heat, melt the 4 tablespoons of butter. Sprinkle in the flour and stir with a wooden spoon until the flour is incorporated, about 1 minute. Gradually add the milk, stirring, and raise the heat to medium. Cook, stirring frequently, until almost boiling and smooth, about 5 minutes. Add the cheeses and stir until melted and incorporated, 2 to 3 minutes. Stir in the pastrami and lower the heat. Add the pasta and season with the salt and pepper.

4. Transfer the pasta to the baking dish and top with the cracker crumbs. Bake until browned and bubbling, 20 to 25 minutes.

Baked Macaroni with White Cheddar Cheese and Cremini Mushrooms

MAKES 4 TO 6 SERVINGS

Smooth and hearty, with the earthy accent of mushrooms, this is a perfect autumn Mac and Cheese from the chef of New York's Grange Hall. It's the one to make when you've found some great creminis at the greenmarket or your local greengrocer.

16 tablespoons canola oil, plus additional for the baking dish

2 slices white bread (fresh or stale)

1/2 cup (2 ounces) grated Grana Padano cheese, or substitute grated Parmigiano-Reggiano cheese

1/2 pound cremini mushrooms, washed, dried, and sliced 1/8 inch thick

1 pound ziti

6 rounded tablespoons flour

2 cups whole milk

1 1/2 cups (6 ounces) shredded sharp white Cheddar cheese

Kosher salt

Freshly ground pepper

1/2 tablespoon dry mustard

1. Preheat the oven to 375°F. Oil a 9 by 13-inch baking dish or ovenproof casserole.

2. Toast the bread in the oven until golden, 4 to 5 minutes, and allow to cool. Break into chunks, chop into crumbs in a food processor, and mix with the Grana Padano; reserve the mixture.

3. In a large sauté pan over medium heat, heat 4 tablespoons of the canola oil until very hot and sauté the mushrooms until fully cooked, about 5 minutes, stirring often. Remove from the heat and place in a strainer to drain and cool.

4. Bring 6 quarts of salted water to a boil with 4 tablespoons of the canola oil. Add the pasta and cook, stirring occasionally to prevent sticking, until al dente, 8 to 10 minutes. Drain and reserve.

5. In a large saucepan over medium heat, heat the remaining 8 tablespoons of canola oil until moderately hot and whisk in the flour. Cook, whisking constantly, until lightly golden brown, about 5 minutes. Raise the heat and slowly whisk in the milk; cook, whisking, until it comes to a boil. Whisk in the Cheddar until well blended. Add the salt, pepper, and mustard and cook, stirring constantly, until the mixture thickens—it will get quite thick (it starts to thicken as soon as you add the milk, so this part takes only a few minutes). Remove from the heat, add the ziti and mushrooms, and stir until well coated.

6. Pour the macaroni mixture into the prepared baking dish and top with the bread crumb mixture. Bake on the middle shelf until bubbling and the top is golden, about 20 minutes.

Macaroni with Duck Prosciutto, Chanterelles, and Mascarpone

MAKES 4 TO 6 SERVINGS

After growing up with his mother's classic Mac and Cheese with Tomatoes (page 38), Tucson's Chef Wilder (of Janos and J Bar) sought new worlds to conquer. His inspired version combines rich mascarpone cheese, duck prosciutto, fresh chanterelles, basil, and "Sweet 100" tomatoes (so tiny that they come 100 to a pint).

Imaginative, restorative, and summery, this is an irresistible dish.

Butter for the baking dish

1 pound elbow macaroni

1 tablespoon olive oil

3 tablespoons chopped garlic

¼ pound chanterelle mushrooms, thickly sliced

1 cup dry white wine

3 tablespoons chopped shallots

1 cup heavy cream

¼ pound mascarpone cheese

1 cup (¼ pound) coarsely grated Parmigiano-Reggiano cheese

About 3 cups firmly packed shredded basil leaves

5 ounces thinly sliced duck prosciutto, coarsely chopped, or substitute regular prosciutto

2 ounces yellow Sweet 100 tomatoes, whole; or substitute slightly larger tomatoes, such as grape, halved

2 ounces red Sweet 100 tomatoes, whole; or substitute slightly larger tomatoes, such as grape, halved

1 cup (¼ pound) grated sharp New York Cheddar cheese

Kosher salt

Freshly ground pepper

1. Preheat the oven to 375°F. Butter a 9 by 13-inch or a 4-quart deep baking dish.

2. Bring a large pot of salted water to a boil over high heat and cook the pasta until al dente, 8 to 10 minutes. Drain and place in a large mixing bowl.

3. In a small skillet over medium-high heat, heat the olive oil until very hot and add 1 tablespoon of the garlic and the chanterelles. Sauté until the garlic is golden and the mushrooms are softened but not colored, about 4 minutes, and reserve.

4. Combine the wine, the remaining garlic, and the shallots in a medium saucepan over medium-high heat and reduce by about three fourths, 6 to 8 minutes. Add the cream and reduce by half, about 5 minutes. Lower the heat to medium and whisk in the mascarpone and Parmigiano-Reggiano, until the cheese is melted and well blended.

5. Add the basil and immediately transfer the mascarpone sauce to a blender or food processor. Puree the sauce (which will be a delicate green, with small bits of basil), and reserve.

6. In the mixing bowl, combine the macaroni, duck prosciutto, mushrooms, tomatoes, half the Cheddar, and the mascarpone sauce. Adjust the seasonings. Pour into the baking dish and top with the remaining Cheddar. Bake on the middle shelf until browned, 35 to 40 minutes.

Baked Cellentani with Four Cheeses, Prosciutto, Artichoke Hearts, and Portobellos

MAKES 4 SERVINGS

This modern take on Italian cuisine from the chefs at Empire, in Providence, Rhode Island, is chock-full of welcoming textures and bright contrasts. There are layers of flavor: savory, herbal, earthy, and, especially, pasta-and-cheesy.

2 tablespoons pure olive oil

4 thin slices prosciutto cotto (cooked prosciutto) or good-quality ham

10 tablespoons butter

2 cups whole milk, plus an extra $1/4$ cup if desired

3 tablespoons flour

1 bay leaf

Kosher salt

$3/4$ pound cellentani or other tubular pasta such as penne, cavatappi, or elbow macaroni

3 tablespoons extra-virgin olive oil

2 medium portobello mushrooms, caps only (about $1/4$ pound), cleaned well and sliced about $1/4$ inch wide and 1 inch long

1 cup ($1/4$ pound) finely grated fresh caciocavallo cheese

$1/4$ pound Bel Paese cheese, crumbled (1 cup)

$1/4$ pound fresh mozzarella cheese, cut into $1/2$-inch cubes (1 cup)

4 good-quality Italian artichoke hearts in olive oil, rinsed and sliced thin

$1/4$ pound Italian sweet sausage meat, removed from casing, browned, and cooled, optional

Freshly ground pepper

2 tablespoons dried bread crumbs

2 tablespoons coarsely chopped flat-leaf parsley

1 teaspoon finely chopped fresh rosemary

1 teaspoon finely chopped fresh thyme

Parmigiano-Reggiano cheese, for grating

97

MAC AND CHEESE TODAY

1. Brush a cookie sheet with 1 tablespoon of the pure olive oil. Lay the prosciutto cotto slices on the sheet and brush with the remaining tablespoon of pure olive oil. Cover and set aside.

2. Smear the inside of a large, ovenproof casserole (about 9 by 13 inches; or 8 inches round, 3 inches deep) with 1 tablespoon of the butter and set aside.

3. Preheat the oven to 400°F.

4. To make the béchamel sauce: In a small saucepan over low heat, bring 2 cups of the milk to a scald and remove from the heat. In another small saucepan, melt 4 tablespoons of the butter over medium-low heat, sprinkle in the flour, and stir with a wooden spoon until the mixture begins to bubble. Continue to cook, stirring constantly, for 1 minute. Slowly pour in the hot milk, whisking constantly. When all the milk has been added, continue to cook, whisking frequently, until the sauce boils. Remove from the heat, add the bay leaf, and season to taste with salt. Pour into a small bowl, cover the surface with plastic wrap (to prevent a skin from forming), and set aside to cool.

5. In a large pot over high heat, bring 3 quarts of salted water to a boil. Add the pasta and cook until al dente, for 1 minute less than the recommended cooking time. Drain and toss with the extra-virgin olive oil. Set aside to cool.

6. In a sauté pan over high heat, melt the remaining 5 tablespoons of butter. Add the sliced mushrooms and sprinkle with a little salt. Reduce the heat to medium and cook, stirring occasionally, until the mushrooms are brown and soft, about 10 minutes. Drain off any excess liquid.

7. In a large bowl, combine the caciocavallo, Bel Paese, mozzarella, artichoke slices, cooked sausage meat (if using), sautéed mushrooms, béchamel (removing the bay leaf), and pasta. If you prefer a thinner sauce, add the additional 1/4 cup milk. Mix gently to combine, season with salt and pepper, and pour into the prepared casserole dish. Sprinkle with the bread crumbs, cover loosely with aluminum foil, and bake on the middle shelf until hot in the center, about 20 minutes.

8. Combine the parsley, rosemary, and thyme.

9. Place the uncovered cookie sheet with the prosciutto in the oven and bake until the slices are hot and beginning to brown at the edges, about 10 minutes. At the same time, uncover the casserole and bake until browned, about 10 minutes.

10. Remove the casserole and the ham from the oven. Divide the macaroni among four warmed pasta bowls and grate the Parmigiano-Reggiano generously over each. Top each serving with a slice of prosciutto and sprinkle with the herbs.

Add macaroni alternately with sauce.   Use a fork to distribute cheese sauce thoroughly.

Baked Stuffed Pasta Spirals

Fresh figs add sweetness to this lush blend of flavors and textures, mushrooms lend their rich flavor and aroma, and nuts provide a bit of crunch. A very light cheese sauce brings together all these good things, in an outstanding dish from Chef Jody Adams of the Boston area's Red Clay and Rialto.

Fresh pasta sheets are available at many specialty grocery and pasta shops, but the frozen variety you find in your local supermarket makes an acceptable substitute. Both types come sprinkled with cornmeal to prevent their sticking together in the package; brush off as much as you can before cooking.

6 tablespoons olive oil

1 shallot, minced (about 1 tablespoon)

1 clove garlic, minced (about 1 teaspoon)

3 large portobello mushroom caps (about $2/3$ pound without stems), cut into $1/4$-inch-wide, 1-inch-long slices

Kosher salt

Freshly ground pepper

$1/2$ teaspoon chopped fresh thyme

2 fresh pasta sheets, 8 by 12 inches, or substitute frozen sheets (4 sheets, 8 by 6 inches)

$1/4$ pound fresh spinach, stemmed, washed, and dried

6 fresh Turkish (brown) figs, stems removed, cut into $1/4$-inch slices

6 tablespoons grated Parmesan cheese

2 tablespoons finely chopped toasted walnuts (see Note)

1 cup heavy cream

$1/2$ cup (2 ounces) crumbled Gorgonzola cheese

4 to 6 sprigs fresh thyme, for garnish

1. Heat 2 tablespoons of the olive oil in a large sauté pan over medium heat. Add the shallot and garlic and cook for 3 minutes. Raise the heat to high and add the mushrooms. Season with salt and pepper and cook until tender, about 3 minutes. Add the chopped thyme and toss to mix. Set aside to cool.

2. Have ready a large bowl of ice water. Bring a large pot of water to a boil over high heat and add 1 teaspoon salt per quart. Add the pasta sheets and cook, stirring occasionally and taking care not to break the sheets, until just tender, about 2 minutes. Transfer the pasta to the ice water to cool; drain immediately (if you leave them in the water too long, they will stick together). Pat the sheets dry with paper towels.

3. Brush a board with 1 tablespoon of the olive oil (make sure it is evenly covered, so the pasta gets coated).

4. Lay one pasta sheet on the board. If you are using 8 by 12-inch sheets, cover with half the spinach, leaving a 2-inch border along the long side farthest from you. Season with salt and pepper. Distribute half the mushrooms evenly over the spinach. Sprinkle half the figs, Parmesan, and walnuts over the mushrooms. If you are using the smaller frozen sheets, use $1/2$ tablespoon of olive oil and one fourth of each ingredient for each.

5. Starting with the long edge closest to you, roll the sheet tightly, jelly roll–style, and seal with the uncovered edge. Cut into six even slices. Repeat this process with the remaining pasta sheet (start by brushing the board with oil). The uncut rolls may be wrapped tightly in aluminum foil and refrigerated up to one day.

6. Preheat the oven to 400°F. Brush a small baking sheet with the remaining 2 tablespoons of olive oil and arrange the spirals on the sheet. Bake on the middle shelf until the spinach is cooked and the rolls are heated through, 10 to 15 minutes.

7. Meanwhile, place the heavy cream in a small pot over medium heat and reduce by one fourth, skimming the foam from the surface. Whisk in the Gorgonzola, stirring until completely dissolved. Season with salt and pepper and keep warm over low heat. The sauce will be thin.

8. Divide the sauce among four to six warmed plates and arrange the pasta spirals on top. Garnish with the thyme sprigs and serve immediately.

NOTE: To toast walnuts: Preheat the oven to 350°F. Place the walnuts on a baking sheet in a single layer and bake on the middle shelf until slightly brown and aromatic, 8 to 10 minutes.

ANDREW CARMELLINI

Fontina and White Truffle Macaroni

MAKES 6 TO 8 SERVINGS

From a chef known for his creativity and virtuosity comes a sophisticated and exciting dish. When he studied in Italy, Chef Carmellini, of Manhattan's Café Boulud, learned traditional pasta-making techniques, as well as how to determine which truffles were the best quality. His experience and skill are evident here.

1 pound penne	2 tablespoons white truffle oil (see Sources)
6 tablespoons butter, plus extra for the baking dish	Kosher salt
1 quart whole milk	Freshly ground pepper
4 sprigs fresh thyme	1/3 cup (about 1 1/2 ounces) freshly grated Parmigiano-Reggiano cheese
1 fresh bay leaf (you may substitute dry)	3 tablespoons fresh bread crumbs
1 small onion (about 1/2 pound), finely chopped	3 ounces fresh white truffle (1 or 2 small pieces; see Sources)
3 tablespoons flour	
1 pound fontina cheese (preferably from Val d'Aosta, Italy), cut into small dice	

1. Fill a medium bowl halfway with ice and cold water. Bring a large pot of salted water to a boil over high heat and cook the pasta until al dente, 10 to 12 minutes. Drain the pasta and transfer to the bowl of ice water. When cool, drain again.

2. Preheat the oven to 450°F. Lightly butter a 3 1/2-quart ovenproof baking dish.

3. In a medium saucepan, combine the milk with the thyme and bay leaf and bring to a scald over medium heat; remove from the heat.

4. In a medium sauté pan over medium heat, melt the 6 tablespoons of butter and cook the onion, stirring occasionally, until soft and translucent, 5 to 7 minutes. Sprinkle with the flour and cook, stirring, for 5 minutes. Slowly pour in half of the scalded milk, whisking to combine, and then add the remaining milk. Simmer for 5 minutes, whisking occasionally, and strain into a clean saucepan. Remove the thyme sprigs and bay leaf. Return to the stove over medium-low heat.

5. Fold the diced fontina cheese into the milk mixture and stir often until all the cheese is melted. Add the white truffle oil and season with salt and pepper (this is the béchamel sauce).

6. Toss the penne with three fourths of the béchamel sauce and transfer to the prepared baking dish. Drizzle the remaining sauce over the top and sprinkle with the grated Parmigiano-Reggiano and the bread crumbs. Cover loosely with aluminum foil and bake until bubbly, about 20 minutes. Remove from the oven, preheat the broiler, and place the uncovered dish under the broiler until crisp and golden brown, about 2 minutes.

7. Divide the fontina macaroni among six to eight warm dinner plates and shave the truffles generously over each serving.

Pasta with Fonduta and Fresh Truffles

MAKES 8 SERVINGS

Imagine a silken, rich Penne Alfredo with truffles. Yes, you have arrived in paradise—or perhaps Farallon restaurant in San Francisco.

Chef Franz advises you to take care with this gorgeous dish. The fonduta (fontina sauce) needs to be cooked very slowly so the eggs don't curdle—a double boiler helps, although it's not really necessary. Fresh chopped black truffles are preferred, but canned truffle peelings are passable (a 1$\frac{1}{2}$-ounce jar of truffle carpaccio, or shaved truffles, is available at many gourmet shops).

Shave fresh black truffles, as much as your budget allows, over the pasta before serving. Fresh white Italian truffles in season are the ultimate luxury, but they should be used only as a garnish—they lose all their flavor and aroma when heated.

1 pound penne, fusilli, or ziti

2 cups heavy cream

4 egg yolks

4 cups (1 pound) shredded Italian fontina cheese

4 tablespoons butter

1 whole fresh black truffle, chopped, or 2 tablespoons canned truffle peelings, plus 1 whole fresh black or white truffle for garnish, optional (see Sources)

Freshly ground pepper

Freshly grated nutmeg

1. Set the oven to 150°F (warm) and put in eight individual rimmed bowls.
2. Bring a large pot of salted water to a boil over high heat and cook the pasta until al dente, 10 to 12 minutes. Drain, reserving 1 or 2 tablespoons of the pasta water. Place the reserved water and the pasta in a large mixing bowl.

3. In a medium, heavy-bottomed saucepan, whisk together the cream and egg yolks. Put the saucepan over low heat and add the cheese and butter. Cook carefully, stirring constantly, until the cheese melts and the mixture has thickened. The sauce can also be made in the top of a double boiler set over, but not touching, simmering water. Some water may boil away; replace with hot tap water. (The sauce can be made up to a day ahead, refrigerated, and then reheated in a low microwave or in a double boiler over simmering water.)

4. Add about 1 cup of the warm sauce and the chopped truffle to the pasta in the bowl and toss to combine. Season with freshly ground pepper.

5. Divide the pasta among the eight warmed bowls and ladle the remaining sauce on top. Sprinkle with nutmeg and, if you wish, shave the remaining truffle over the dish for garnish.

ONE c.p.s. Wild Mushroom and Truffle Macaroni and Cheese

MAKES 6 TO 8 SERVINGS

This dish is based on the macaroni and cheese tart served at Chef Burke's celebrated restaurant on Central Park South in New York City. It is infused with rich mushroom flavor, along with the luxurious notes of truffle butter, truffle oil, and shavings of the earthy diamonds themselves. But it is still Mac and Cheese—an extraordinary blend of haute cuisine and country cooking.

1 pound ditalini	2 cups (1/2 pound) mascarpone cheese
Butter for the tartlet pans	1/2 cup (2 ounces) grated Parmigiano-Reggiano cheese
1 pound mixed wild mushrooms, cleaned, stems removed and reserved	2 tablespoons truffle butter (see Sources)
2 cups chicken stock or canned low-sodium broth	1 tablespoon truffle oil (see Sources)
1/4 cup chopped dried porcini mushrooms	Kosher salt
1 tablespoon clarified butter (see Note)	Freshly ground white pepper
2 shallots, minced	1/2 pound raclette cheese, in 1 piece
1 teaspoon minced garlic	1/4 cup fresh truffle shavings

1. Bring a large pot of salted water to a boil over high heat and cook the ditalini until al dente, about 11 minutes. Drain and cool.

2. Preheat the broiler. Generously butter six to eight individual tartlet pans and set aside.

3. Coarsely chop the mushroom caps and set aside.

4. Place the chicken stock in a medium saucepan over medium-high heat and add the dried porcini and the mushroom stems. Bring to a simmer; lower the heat and simmer until the stock is nicely infused with mushroom flavor, about 15 minutes. Remove from the heat and drain the liquid through a fine sieve lined with cheesecloth (or a double thickness of paper towels) into a clean bowl, discarding the solids. Set aside.

5. Heat the clarified butter in a large saucepan over medium heat. Add the shallots, garlic, and chopped mushroom caps and sauté until softened, 8 to 10 minutes.

6. Add the reserved mushroom stock, raise the heat to high, and bring to a boil. Immediately add the ditalini and stir to combine. Lower the heat to medium and stir in the mascarpone cheese, Parmigiano-Reggiano, truffle butter, and truffle oil. Stir to incorporate and season to taste with salt and white pepper. Pour an equal portion of the ditalini mixture into each prepared tartlet pan.

7. Using a cheese shaver (or a vegetable peeler, or the large slicing ridge on a box grater), shave a generous helping of raclette cheese over the top of each tartlet. Immediately place under the broiler until the cheese is melting, lightly browned, and bubbly, 3 to 4 minutes. Remove from the heat and sprinkle truffle shavings over the top of each tartlet. Serve very hot.

NOTE: To clarify butter: Melt the butter in a small pot over medium-low heat. Pour off the clear liquid (the clarified butter) and discard the solids that remain.

Baked Conchiglie with Roasted Garlic– Cheese Sauce, Ricotta Cheese, and White Truffle Oil

MAKES 4 TO 6 SERVINGS

The shells provide a great hiding place for cheese or a piece of garlic, so when you bite into each piece of pasta, you may be pleasantly surprised. Because the garlic has been roasted, it is sweet and subtle, and doesn't overwhelm the other flavors in this luscious dish from the chef of New York's Mesa Grill and Bolo.

1 head garlic

Olive oil, for rubbing the garlic

4 tablespoons butter, plus extra for the baking dish

1 pound conchiglie (medium shells)

2½ cups whole milk

1 medium onion (⅓ to ½ pound), finely diced

3 tablespoons flour

1 cup (¼ pound) grated mozzarella or fontina cheese

1 cup (½ pound) whole-milk ricotta cheese, drained

Kosher salt

Freshly ground pepper

½ cup (2 ounces) grated Parmigiano-Reggiano cheese

2 tablespoons white truffle oil (see Sources)

1. Preheat the oven to 300°F. Cut off the bud end and rub the head of garlic with olive oil. Wrap loosely in foil, place on a baking pan, and roast until very soft, 45 minutes to 1 hour. Peel, or squeeze out the softened garlic, and mash (can be refrigerated up to one day).

2. Raise the oven temperature to 375°F. Butter a 9 by 13-inch baking dish.

3. Meanwhile, bring 6 quarts of salted water to a boil. Add the pasta and cook, stirring occasionally, until al dente, about 13 minutes. Drain and reserve.

4. In a small saucepan over medium heat, bring the milk to a scald.

5. In a medium saucepan over medium heat, melt the 4 tablespoons of butter. Add the onion and cook until softened, about 5 minutes. Reduce the heat to low and whisk in the flour; cook, whisking, about 2 minutes, not allowing it to color. Whisk in the hot milk a little at a time. Once all the milk has been added, raise the heat to medium and cook, stirring occasionally, until the sauce thickens slightly. Whisk in the roasted garlic and the grated mozzarella and continue whisking until blended. Remove from the heat.

6. Add the cooked pasta and the ricotta to the roasted garlic–cheese sauce and stir to combine. Season with salt and pepper. Pour or spoon the mixture into the buttered baking dish and sprinkle the Parmigiano-Reggiano evenly over the top. Bake until the top is golden brown, about 25 minutes. Remove from the oven and drizzle with the truffle oil. Let rest for 5 minutes before serving, so the dish can absorb the truffle flavor.

California Truffled Macaroni and Cheese

MAKES 6 SERVINGS

Tim Goodell assures us that when people order generous servings of his Mac and Cheese for lunch at his restaurants, Aubergine, Troquet, and Red Pearl Kitchen, they don't order more food—they have no room for anything else. It is uncomplicated, yet elegant, perfectly spiced, and satisfying.

4 tablespoons butter, plus extra for the baking dish

1 pound elbow macaroni

2 quarts whole milk

½ cup flour

½ tablespoon minced garlic

½ pound sharp Cheddar cheese, cut into ¼-inch dice

¼ pound Montgomery Cheddar cheese (or substitute a mild Cheddar), cut into ¼-inch dice

2 ounces Gorgonzola cheese, crumbled

½ teaspoon Tabasco

1 teaspoon black truffle oil (see Sources)

Kosher salt

Freshly ground pepper

½ cup (2 ounces) grated Parmigiano-Reggiano cheese

¼ cup panko (Japanese bread crumbs)

Fresh chives, for garnish

1. Preheat the oven to 350°F. Lightly butter a 9 by 13-inch baking dish and set on a foil-lined sheet pan (to catch any spills).

2. Bring a large pot of salted water to a boil over high heat and cook the pasta until al dente, 8 to 10 minutes. Drain.

3. In a large saucepan over medium-high heat, heat the milk until almost scalding.

4. In a large saucepan over medium-low heat, melt the 4 tablespoons of butter, add the flour, and cook, stirring occasionally, until smooth and straw-colored, about 3 minutes. Raise the heat to medium, whisk the hot milk into the flour mixture, and continue whisking until smooth. Slowly bring to a boil, stirring occasionally to make sure that the milk at the bottom doesn't burn, and remove from the heat. Add the garlic and sharp Cheddar, Montgomery Cheddar, and Gorgonzola cheeses and mix carefully. Add the Tabasco and truffle oil and season with salt and pepper. Stir in the cooked macaroni.

5. Pour into the prepared baking dish. Combine the grated Parmigiano-Reggiano and the panko crumbs and sprinkle over the macaroni mixture. Bake until bubbling and browned, 15 to 20 minutes. Garnish individual servings with chives.

Chunks of Lobster Swimming in Cheesy Macaroni

MAKES 4 TO 6 SERVINGS

The chef of Norma's at New York's Le Parker Meridien Hotel gives us a recipe that is as sumptuous and sublime as it sounds. Think of Alex Porter's luxurious combination of lobster and creamy cheeses when you plan your New Year's Eve menu, or any time you deserve a bit of pampering.

1 pound elbow macaroni	Freshly grated nutmeg
2 cups heavy cream	Dash of Tabasco, optional
1¼ cups (5 ounces) coarsely grated sharp Cheddar cheese	2 tablespoons butter
	1 small onion, finely chopped (about ½ cup)
1 cup (¼ pound) coarsely grated Monterey Jack cheese	5 lobster tails (¼ pound each), shelled and cut into bite-size pieces (see Note)
¾ cup (3 ounces) coarsely grated blue cheese	1 cup white wine
Kosher salt	1¼ cups (5 ounces) coarsely grated Gruyère cheese
Freshly ground pepper	

1. Bring a large pot of salted water to a boil over high heat and cook the pasta until al dente, 8 to 10 minutes. Drain and reserve.

2. Preheat the oven to 350°F.

3. In a large (3½- to 4-quart) saucepan over medium heat, bring the cream to a boil and reduce it by half, watching closely so it doesn't boil over. Reduce the heat to low and stir in the Cheddar, Mon-

terey Jack, and blue cheese and simmer, stirring constantly, until melted. Season with salt, pepper, nutmeg, and Tabasco, if desired. Turn off the heat and let sit, stirring occasionally.

4. In a large skillet over medium heat, melt the butter and sauté the onion until translucent, about 6 minutes. Add the lobster pieces and stir to combine. Add the wine, raise the heat to medium-high, and bring to a boil. Reduce the heat to medium or medium-low and cook, stirring occasionally, until the wine has evaporated (about 30 minutes). Remove from the heat.

5. Add the cooked macaroni and the cheese mixture to the lobster mixture, stir to combine, and divide among four to six shallow, ovenproof bowls, or pour into a 9 by 13-inch baking pan. Top with the Gruyère and bake until the sauce is bubbly and the top is golden and crusty, 15 to 20 minutes.

NOTE: Lobster tails are available frozen. Ask the fishmonger to crack the shell—it will be easier to remove the meat. You can defrost the tails overnight in the fridge or place them in a bowl and run a steady stream of cold water over them until they are completely thawed.

Joseph's Table Mac and Cheese with Dried Cherry Chutney and Roquefort Sauce

MAKES 4 TO 6 SERVINGS

Joseph is known for his inspired combinations, as the following dish makes abundantly clear. Creamy Roquefort sauce mellows out the potent flavors of the chutney, but that is only the beginning: endive adds crunch with a hint of bitterness and crumbled bacon provides savory crispness. Add all these to Mac and Cheese and you are soaring.

FOR THE DRIED CHERRY CHUTNEY
(Makes about 2 cups)

1 cup champagne vinegar

1 cup sugar

1 tablespoon ground mustard seeds

½ cup chopped onion

½ cup tomato concasse (see page 116)

½ cup peeled and finely diced ginger

½ cup dried cherries

Combine all the ingredients in a medium saucepan over medium-high heat and cook, stirring occasionally, until the liquid has evaporated, 20 to 25 minutes. Be careful not to burn. It will be very thick, like jam. (May be made up to two days ahead and refrigerated, covered.)

FOR THE ROQUEFORT SAUCE
(Makes about 1¹/₂ cups)

3 cups heavy cream

1 cup apple cider

1 cup (¹/₄ pound) crumbled Roquefort cheese

Freshly ground pepper

In a large saucepan over medium-high heat, combine all the ingredients and bring to a boil. Lower the heat to medium and simmer until reduced by half (about 45 minutes).

TO ASSEMBLE THE DISH

1 pound elbow macaroni

Butter or oil for the baking dish

3 heads (about 1 pound) Belgian endive, cleaned and sliced into thin circles

1 pound bacon, cooked until crisp, drained, and crumbled (use your favorite method—stovetop, oven, or microwave)

Kosher salt

Fresh-cracked black pepper (see Note)

---

1. Preheat the oven to 350°F.
2. Bring a large pot of salted water to a boil over high heat and cook the macaroni until al dente, 8 to 10 minutes. Drain.
3. Butter a 3¹/₂-quart deep baking dish or a 9 by 13-inch baking pan and pour the macaroni into it. Distribute the endive, chutney, and bacon evenly over the top and pour the Roquefort sauce over all. Season with salt and pepper. Bake on the middle shelf until golden brown and bubbling, about 25 minutes.

NOTE: For cracked black pepper, wrap peppercorns in a dish towel and smash them with a heavy pan.

TO MAKE 1/2 CUP TOMATO CONCASSE

1 medium ripe tomato, cored, with a small X cut on the bottom

Bring a small pot of lightly salted water to a boil and immerse the tomato for 10 to 15 seconds. Remove from the water and peel—the skin should slip off easily. Cut in half and squeeze gently to remove the seeds and juice. Cut the flesh into 1/4-inch dice.

Sweetened Mascarpone and Noodle Pudding

MAKES 4 SERVINGS

A dreamy spin on Mac and Cheese, this orangy custard dessert uses just a sprinkle of pasta to provide a bit of texture. With both pasta and cheese on the ingredients list, it fits our requirements, but the result is a surprise—sweet, refined, and rarefied.

1/2 teaspoon plus 1 pinch kosher salt	1 tablespoon coarsely chopped lemon zest
2 tablespoons (1 ounce) soup-style pasta, such as ditali ligati, farfalline, pastina, or alphabets	1 tablespoon coarsely chopped orange zest
1 teaspoon granulated sugar	1 vanilla bean
1/4 cup whole milk	1 egg plus 3 egg yolks
1 1/2 cups heavy cream	1/4 cup (2 ounces) mascarpone cheese
1/4 cup plus 2 tablespoons powdered sugar	Fresh seasonal fruits, sliced or cubed, for serving

1. Preheat the oven to 275°F. Have ready an 8-inch round (or square), 3-inch-deep baking dish set into a larger dish.

2. In a medium pot over high heat, bring 1 quart of water to a boil with the 1/2 teaspoon of salt. Add the pasta and cook until al dente—1 minute less than the shortest cooking time given on the package. Drain, using a cheesecloth-lined colander if the pasta is smaller than the colander holes. Toss with the granulated sugar and set aside to cool.

117

3. In a medium, heavy-bottomed stainless steel saucepan, combine the milk, cream, powdered sugar, lemon and orange zests, and the remaining pinch of salt. Split the vanilla bean and scrape the seeds into the milk mixture, along with the pod. Bring to a scald over medium heat. Remove from the heat and allow the mixture to steep uncovered for 20 minutes.

4. Combine the egg, egg yolks, and mascarpone in a stainless steel bowl and whisk until the mixture is smooth.

5. Strain the milk mixture into a small pot, discard the solids, and return the liquid to the stove. Warm it over medium heat until the mixture just begins to bubble; do not allow it to boil. Begin whisking the egg mixture, and gently drizzle some of the hot milk mixture into it. Continue gradually adding and whisking until one third of the milk mixture is incorporated; then pour the warmed egg mixture back into the milk, whisking as you pour. Strain the milk mixture into a clean stainless steel bowl or a measuring cup large enough to accommodate all the custard (you will have about $2^{1}/_{3}$ cups).

6. Spread the cooked pasta on the bottom of the smaller baking dish and pour the warm custard over it. Stir to fully coat the pasta. Pour warm water into the outer baking dish to come $1^{1}/_{2}$ to 2 inches up the outside of the smaller dish (don't use boiling water—it will start to cook the eggs). Bake uncovered on the middle shelf until slightly firm and golden, 30 to 45 minutes. Remove from the oven and allow to cool in the water bath for 15 minutes. Divide the pudding among four dessert plates and serve warm with fresh fruit.

You will find almost everything you need at your local ethnic and gourmet markets, farmers' markets, and fine supermarkets. Here are some telephone and Internet sources, as well.

ARTISANAL PASTA

www.flyingnoodle.com

www.chefshop.com

Earthy Delights: www.earthy.com

CHEESES

Murray's Cheese Shop and Murray's by Mail catalogue: 888-692-4339;

e-mail: murray's_cheese@msn.com

Mediterranean Foods (Greek feta cheese): 718-728-6166;

www.mediterraneanfoods-inc.com

TRUFFLES, TRUFFLE PRODUCTS, AND WILD MUSHROOMS

Urbani USA: 718-392-5050; www.urbaniusa.com

Earthy Delights: www.earthy.com

Dean & DeLuca: 800-221-7714; www.deandeluca.com

Oakshire Mushroom Farm: 800-255-2077; www.mushroomlovers.com

Marché aux Délices: 888-547-5471; www.auxdelices.com

D'Artagnan: 800-327-8246; www.d'artagnan.com

RAMPS

Earthy Delights: www.earthy.com

ALEPPO PEPPER

Kalustyan's: 212-685-3451; www.kalustyans.com

Adriana's Caravan: 800-316-0820

Dean & DeLuca: 800-221-7714; www.deandeluca.com

RAS EL HANOUT

Adriana's Caravan: 800-316-0820

FOIE GRAS

Urbani USA: 718-392-5050; www.urbaniusa.com

Dean & DeLuca: 800-221-7714; www.deandeluca.com

D'Artagnan: 800-327-8246; www.d'artagnan.com

JODY ADAMS, chef and partner of Rialto in Cambridge, and Red Clay in Chestnut Hill, Massachusetts, is known for her exciting combinations of New England ingredients with Mediterranean culinary traditions. Her passion for food began at her family's dinner table and was fueled by her time living and traveling in Europe. As a talented and veteran chef in Boston, Jody has received many honors throughout the years. In 1997 she won the James Beard Award for Best Chef: Northeast, and in *Gourmet* magazine's October 2000 restaurant issue, Rialto was ranked "#1 Restaurant in Boston." She and her husband, Ken Rivard, are writing a cookbook.

JEFFREY BANK AND CHRIS METZ are co-owners of Artie's New York Delicatessen, named in honor of the late restaurateur Arthur Cutler, an original planner of the venture. They also collaborated on Abigael's Grill and the King David Delicatessen.

Jeffrey, who has a degree in political science from the State University of New York at Albany, had planned to study law but happily discovered his calling the summer after he graduated from college. Chris, a graduate of Syracuse University, worked with chefs Anne Rosenzweig and Phil McGrath and went on to study at London's Cordon Bleu Cooking School. Their restaurant is a re-creation of a 1930s-style Jewish deli. They are most proud of their home-cured pastrami, created from a secret recipe.

RICK BAYLESS is the chef and owner of Chicago's famous Frontera Grill and Topolobampo. Born into an Oklahoma City family of restaurateurs, he learned about Mexican cooking as an undergraduate student in Spanish and Latin American culture.

Among his many awards are *Food & Wine* magazine, Best New Chef of 1988; James Beard Foundation, Best American Chef: Midwest, 1991; both the Beard Foundation's National Chef of the Year and the International Association of Culinary Professionals Chef of the Year awards, 1995; and the James Beard Foundation's Humanitarian of the Year, 1998. He has been inducted into *Who's Who of American Food and Drink.*

Rick has appeared widely on television and radio, and has written for numerous publications, including *Eating Well, Food & Wine, Vegetarian Times, Travel & Leisure,* and *Saveur,* where he is a contributing editor. His twenty-six-part television series, *Mexico One Plate at a Time,* and the companion book of the same name debuted in 2000. He is chairman of Chefs' Collaborative and is active in Share Our Strength. He is a restaurant consultant, teaches Mexican cooking, and leads cooking and cultural tours to Mexico.

JAMES BOTSACOS, executive chef of Molyvos, in New York City, is a descendant of talented Greek-American and Italian-American chefs and is a graduate of Rhode Island's Johnson and Wales University. At New York's "21" Club, he advanced from summer intern to saucier to sous-chef, and then became executive sous-chef. Also in New York, he was the first executive chef at the Park Avalon and was consulting chef at the Blue Water Grill. In 1997, with his move to Molyvos, he traveled to Greece to research the country's regional home cooking. *The New York Times* awarded Molyvos three stars in 1997, *Esquire* magazine's John Mariani named the restaurant among the "Best in America" that same year, and it made *New York* magazine's "Best of 1999" list.

ANTOINE BOUTERIN, executive chef and owner of Bouterin, on Manhattan's East Side, was born on a historic farm in Saint-Rémy-de-Provence. Although he came from a family of farmers, he decided at the age of twelve to become a chef and soon afterward apprenticed at the two-star Riboto de Taven in Les-Baux-de-Provence. He honed his skills at the celebrated L'Escale, near Marseilles, among other fine restaurants, and moved to Paris, where, despite his youth, he became chef at the fashionable Quai d'Orsay. His next move was to New York's Le Périgord, where he was executive chef from 1982 to 1995.

He then opened the successful Bouterin, filled with the art and food of his native Provence. Chef Bouterin is the author of *Cooking Provence, Cooking with Antoine at Le Périgord,* and *Antoine Bouterin's Desserts from Le Périgord.*

DAVID BURKE, executive chef and partner of the Smith and Wollensky Restaurant Group, created the cuisine at New York's Park Avenue Cafe, Maloney & Porcelli, and ONEc.p.s., as well as at Chicago's Park Avenue Cafe and Mrs. Park's Tavern.

A graduate of the Culinary Institute of America, Chef Burke studied pastry arts at the École Lenôtre in Plasir, France, and worked as a *stagiaire* at a number of renowned French restaurants before returning to the United States. He served as executive chef at the River Café from 1987 to 1991; he then became executive chef and partner at the Park Avenue Cafe.

Among his many honors, Chef Burke was named Chef of the Year by both the Vatel Club and *Chef* magazine in 1998, and won the American Academy of Hospitality Sciences Five-Diamond Award of Excellence. He received the Robert Mondavi Culinary Award of Excellence in 1996 and 1997, and in 1996 he won the CIA's first Auggie Award (named for August Escoffier). In 1991, Chef Burke was named to the National Advisory Committee of Chefs in America and was voted Chef of the Year. In 1988 he won the Meilleurs Ouvriers de France diploma, as well as the Nippon Award of Excellence, in Tokyo.

He is the author of *Cooking with David Burke of the Park Avenue Cafe.*

SCOTT CAMPBELL, executive chef and owner of Avenue, on New York City's Upper West Side, began his career at Detroit's famed London Chop House. Moving to New York, he became sous-chef at the Plaza Hotel's Oak Room, and then studied and taught at Peter Kump's Cooking School. He is a graduate of the first class of the Beringer School of American Chefs in Napa Valley, directed by his longtime mentor, Madeleine Kamman.

He cooked at many high-profile New York restaurants, including Windows on the World, Union Square Café, Le Cirque (with Daniel Boulud), QV (with Joachim Splichal), and Hubert's, and he was the opening chef at Sfuzzi, Lincon Center.

Chef Campbell is a James Beard Foundation Rising Star of American Cuisine and co-chair of its Chefs' Round Table. He is well known for his many charitable activities and was awarded the 1996 Mayor's Certificate for Outstanding Volunteer Services by Mayor Rudolph Giuliani.

ANDREW CARMELLINI, executive chef of New York's Café Boulud, is a graduate of the Culinary Institute of America. During his time at the CIA, he completed *stagiaires* in a series of top Manhattan restaurants and spent his weekends cooking for then governor Mario Cuomo and his family in the governor's mansion in Albany. When Andrew cooked at the three-star San Domenico, owner Tony May sent him to study with Chef Valentino Mercatelli at San Domenico in Italy. Upon his return to the United States, he spent three years at New York's San Domenico and then moved to Gray Kunz's Lespinasse. In 1996, he began a six-month European tour, working in the kitchens of a host of top restaurants. Back home again, he became sous-chef at Le Cirque 2000, and then moved to the new Café Boulud, working under Daniel Boulud. Andrew was named one of America's Ten Best New Chefs of 2000 by *Food & Wine* magazine and received the James Beard Foundation's Perrier-Jouët Rising Star Chef of the Year Award in 2000.

ANDREA CURTO, chef at Wish restaurant in Miami's South Beach, was born in Vero Beach, Florida, and is a graduate of the Culinary Institute of America. Her love of cooking was nurtured by her Italian grandmother. Before Wish, she cooked at Manhattan's Tribeca Grill and The Heights in Coral Gables, Florida. One of *Food & Wine* magazine's Ten Best New Chefs of 2000, Andrea was cited for creating dishes that are bold yet perfectly balanced. *The New York Times* called Wish "one of SoBe's best restaurants."

MITCHELL DAVIS has been the director of publications for the James Beard Foundation since December 1993. During that time, he has moonlighted as a freelance writer, restaurant critic, and cookbook author. Whenever he is feeling overwhelmed by all of his work, or lonely, he makes his favorite Mac and Cheese for himself and tries to finish it all. His books include *Cook Something* and *Foie Gras: A Passion* (co-authored with Michael Ginor), and his latest book will be published in 2002.

His restaurant reviews have appeared in a number of national magazines, including *Food & Wine*, *GQ,* and *Time Out New York.* Mitchell is also working toward a Ph.D. in the Department of Food Studies at New York University. His scholarly work has appeared in the journal *Gastronomica* and has been presented at international food conferences.

JOHN DELUCIE, executive chef of Manhattan's Soho Grand Hotel, is in charge of the celebrated food at Upstairs, Grand Bar & Lounge, catering, and room service. A 1985 graduate of the Gallatin Division of New York University and the master chef program at the New School for the Culinary Arts, John has worked with Andy D'Amico and David Walzog at Arizona 206, Rick Laakonen at Luxe, Rick Moonen at Oceana, and Jonathan Waxman at Colina, among others. He has been a featured chef at the James Beard House and has appeared on television. His cooking has been praised in *The New York Times, The New York Observer,* and *USA Today.*

ROCCO DiSPIRITO, executive chef of Manhattan's innovative Union Pacific restaurant, has been called "America's most exciting young chef" by *Gourmet* magazine. Rocco entered the Culinary Institute of America at age sixteen and, after graduating in 1986, studied classical technique at the prestigious Jardin de Cygne in Paris with Dominique Cécillón. He returned to New York in 1988 to work at Adrienne, at what is now the Peninsula Hotel. He earned a B.A. in business from Boston University in 1990, and later cooked at Aujourd'hui in Boston. Returning to Manhattan, he embarked upon a series of *stagiaires* with the city's leading chefs: David Bouley, Charlie Palmer, Gilbert LeCoze, and Gray Kunz. He then became part of Lespinasse's opening team, and in 1995 opened Dava Restaurant in Manhattan as executive chef. He was named a Best New Chef of 1999 by *Food & Wine* magazine and was nominated for a 1999 James Beard Foundation Award. Chef DiSpirito has been praised for his unique outlook on modern cuisine and his "unbridled chutzpah."

KEITH DRESSER, most recently the sous-chef at Boston's Red Clay, has been cooking on the coast of New England for his entire career. He has been executive chef at the Regatta of Falmouth, Massachusetts, and has cooked at Hamersley's Bistro in Boston's South End and at Eat, in Somerville. He studied at the New England Culinary Institute at Montpelier, Vermont, and at Harvard University.

WYLIE DuFRESNE, chef-owner of 71 Clinton Fresh Food, in the heart of New York's Lower East Side, received his B.A. in philosophy from Colby College in Waterville, Maine, and graduated from the French Culinary Institute. As a student, he worked at Al Forno in Providence, Rhode Island, and the Gotham Bar and Grill in New York. After a *stagiaire* in L'Esperance restaurant in Burgundy, France, he joined Jean-Georges Vongerichten for six years at Jo Jo, as chef at Prime in the Bellagio, Las Vegas, and as sous-chef at Restaurant Jean-Georges in New York.

Wylie was a finalist in the Perrier-Jouët Rising Star Chef of the Year Award for 2000 for the

James Beard Foundation; has been honored by *New York* magazine as one of ten individuals who have positively affected life in the city in the past year; and was named the French Culinary Institute's graduate of the year. *The New Yorker, The New York Observer, The New York Times,* and *Esquire* magazine all have praised his work enthusiastically.

LOREN FALSONE AND ERIC MOSHIER, executive chefs and owners of Empire, in Providence, Rhode Island, are graduates of Johnson and Wales University, where they met. This husband-and-wife team was chosen by *Food & Wine* magazine to be among America's Ten Best New Chefs of 2000, and they have been praised for their inventive interpretations of Italian home cooking. Before opening Empire, Eric and Loren cooked at Al Forno, in Providence, under Johanne Killeen and George Germon.

BOBBY FLAY, chef and partner of Manhattan's popular Mesa Grill and Bolo, began working at Joe Allen's restaurant at the age of seventeen, where he so impressed the management that Joe Allen paid his tuition to the prestigious French Culinary Institute. After working with restaurateur Jonathan Waxman, Bobby moved to New York's Miracle Grill and raised it to near-cult status with his colorful southwestern creations. Bobby's own Mesa Grill opened in 1991, followed by Bolo, dedicated to exploring Spanish cuisine, in 1993.

In 1993, Bobby was voted the James Beard Foundation's Rising Star Chef of the Year, and that same year the French Culinary Institute honored him with its first Outstanding Graduate Award. He is the author of *Bobby Flay's Bold American Food, From My Kitchen to Your Table,* and *Boy Meets Grill.* Bobby is well known to television viewers for his popular shows, *Grillin' and Chillin', The Main Ingredient, Hot Off the Grill,* and *FoodNation.*

MARK FRANZ, executive chef and co-owner of Farallon in San Francisco, is a graduate of the California Culinary Academy and a third-generation restaurateur. He has cooked at Jeremiah Tower's Stars and Balboa Café, the Santa Fe Bar and Grill in Berkeley, and Ernie's in San Francisco. Under his stewardship, Farallon has been nominated by the James Beard Foundation as one of the best restaurants in the United States, has been chosen one of the best newcomers by *Esquire, Bon Appétit,* and *Food & Wine,* and was the highest-rated newcomer in the 1999 *Zagat Survey.*

IRA FREEHOF, founder and owner of New York's two Comfort Diners, is a diner historian and aficionado. He has been part of the New York restaurant scene for many years as manager and director of operations for several well-known and highly successful ventures, including Steak Frites, Chat n' Chew, and Isabella's. Ira and the Comfort Diners have been featured in *Woman's Day, Bon Appétit, Chocolatier, New York, Newsday,* and *The New York Times,* as well as on television and radio.

TIM GOODELL is executive chef and owner of Aubergine, in Newport Beach, Troquet, in Costa Mesa, and Red Pearl Kitchen, in Huntington Beach, California. After graduating from the California Culinary Academy in San Francisco, he honed his skills at the Ritz-Carlton Dining Room in San Francisco and Pascal's in Newport Beach. Tim was voted one of America's Ten Best New Chefs of 2000 by *Food & Wine* magazine, and his cooking was praised for successfully combining French technique with California ingredients.

GORDON HAMERSLEY, chef and owner of Boston's legendary Hamersley's Bistro, began cooking as a student at Boston University in the early 1970s and trained at various local French restaurants. In 1979, he moved to Ma Maison in Los Angeles, where Wolfgang Puck was the chef. In 1983, after spending a year in Nice, he became sous-chef to Chef Lydia Shire at the Boston Hotel.

In 1987, Chef Hamersley and his wife, Fiona, opened Hamersley's Bistro, serving traditional French-inspired bistro food as well as contemporary American dishes cooked with New England ingredients. He won the James Beard Award for Best Chef: Northeast in 1995 and was named one of *Food & Wine* magazine's Ten Best New Chefs for 1988. Hamersley's Bistro was named Best of Boston by *Boston* magazine from 1988 through 1995, and in 1996 won the magazine's Hall of Fame award. In 1997, *The Boston Globe* awarded Hamersley's Bistro four stars.

Gordon appeared on Julia Child's television series *Cooking with Master Chefs* and is included in the cookbook of the same name. He is a member of the American Institute of Food and Wine and Chefs' Collaborative 2000.

LESLIE HOLLEY-McKEN, a caterer and graduate of the New York Restaurant School, inherited the love and skills of cooking from her mother, Pearl. A weaver and textile designer as well as an innovative chef, Leslie has a bachelor's degree in fine art. She was chef at Brooklyn's New Prospect at Home before founding In Good Taste, her catering firm in Laurelton, Queens.

KEVIN JOHNSON, head chef and partner of The Grange Hall in Greenwich Village, has had over eighteen years of diverse cooking experience. He collaborated on the start-ups of Café Artiste and Savoy, in Louisville, Kentucky, as well as Sugar Reef, in Manhattan's East Village, and has had catering and corporate dining experience. At The Grange Hall, whose motto is "Food from the American Farm," he creates a unique style of contemporary American food with traditional heartland references.

MELISSA KELLY, executive chef and co-owner of Primo, in Rockland, Maine, was named Best Chef: Northeast by the James Beard Foundation in 1999. She won attention as executive chef of the widely praised Old Chatham Sheepherding Company Inn in Upstate New York and has been featured in *The New York Times, The Boston Globe, Gourmet, Bon Appétit, Art Culinaire, New York* magazine, and many other publications. *Food & Wine* voted her one of the Upcoming Chefs of the 1990s, and *Nation's Restaurant News* named her one of 2000's New Taste-Makers. She grew up on Long Island, working in the family garden, fishing, and learning about cooking from her Italian grandmother. Chef Kelly graduated first in her class from the Culinary Institute of America.

MATTHEW KENNEY is executive chef and owner of Matthew's, Mezze, Canteen, and Commune, all in New York City; Commune, in Atlanta; Commissary, in Portland, Maine; and Nickerson Tavern, in Searsport, Maine. He is a graduate of the French Culinary Institute and in 1995 was granted its Outstanding Graduate Award, as well as being named PBS Rising Star Chef. In 1994 and 1995, he was nominated for the James Beard Foundation's Rising Star Chef Award, and he was recognized by *Food & Wine* magazine in 1994 as one of the Ten Best New Chefs in America. He is the author of *Matthew Kenney's Mediterranean Cooking* and *Big City Cooking*.

MITCHEL LONDON, owner of Mitchel London Foods, a prepared foods, catering, and pastry shop with three branches in Manhattan, is a graduate of and former teacher at the Rhode Island School of Design's Culinary Arts School. He served for seven years as chef to Mayor Ed Koch and is the author of

Mitchel London's Gracie Mansion Cookbook. In addition to retail and catering, Mitchel London Foods is a purveyor of pastries to fine food emporiums such as Dean & DeLuca and Balducci's. Mitchel also acts as a consultant to the prepared foods, pastry, and café departments of Fairway Market in New York City.

WALDY MALOUF, chef and co-owner of the Beacon restaurants in Manhattan and Stamford, Connecticut, graduated from the Culinary Institute of America in 1975, winning first prize in the Carras Culinary Competition. His extensive professional experience includes affiliations with the Four Seasons, La Côte Basque, the St. Regis Hotel, the Hudson River Club, and the Rainbow Room, all in New York City, and La Crémaillère, in Banksville, New York.

Chef Malouf has been featured in *Metropolitan Home, New York, Ladies' Home Journal,* and *Food & Wine,* among other publications, and has made many television appearances. He is currently developing a thirteen-part travel and food series for PBS. His *The Hudson River Valley Cookbook* was nominated for a Julia Child Award from the International Association of Culinary Professionals (IACP) and was named one of the year's ten best cookbooks by *The New York Times Book Review.* He was honored at the CIA 1996 Golden Anniversary Gala and has been named a Great Chef of New York numerous times by the James Beard Foundation. In 1997 he was inducted into the *Nation's Restaurant News* Hall of Fame.

HENRY ARCHER MEER made an early career choice, and his classical training at the Culinary Institute of America led him to the legendary La Côte Basque, where he worked for over eight years. He then moved to Lutèce and cooked alongside Chef André Soltner for ten years, the last four as sous-chef. He opened SoHo's Cub Room in 1994 and in 1998 created City Hall restaurant—the quintessential New York eatery—in a landmark Tribeca building. Here he has re-created classic New York cuisine and added a clever, contemporary twist.

Chef Meer works with farmers in the tri-state area to strengthen the important farm/restaurant relationship, and participates in Chefs' Collaborative 2000 and the Council of the Environment for the City of New York, which operates the local greenmarkets.

JOSÉ ARTURO MOLINA, executive chef at New York's Chat n' Chew restaurant, was born and raised in Guayaquil, Ecuador, where his father was a jeweler. A self-taught cook, Chef Molina started in the restaurant business as a dishwasher and rose to the position of chef. He previously worked at Manhattan's Sporting Club. He has been praised for his creativity and unique treatment of pastas and seafood dishes.

MICHAEL O'NEILL, executive chef at Fairway Market in New York City, is a 1979 graduate of the prestigious Le Cordon Bleu cooking school in Paris. He has worked in Boston's Parker House; the Contemporary Hotel in Disney World, Orlando; and the exclusive Starlight Country Inn in Pennsylvania.

CHARLIE PALMER is chef-owner of Aureole, Alva, Métrazur, and Lenox in New York City; Astra in New York and Los Angeles; Aureole and Charlie Palmer Steak at the Four Seasons in Las Vegas; and Hotel Healdsburg and Dry Creek Kitchen in Sonoma, California. Chef Palmer was raised on a farm in Upstate New York. A graduate of the Culinary Institute of America, he cooked at La Côte Basque and the Waccabuc Country Club before becoming executive chef at the River Café, which he raised to three-star status. At age twenty-eight, he opened the highly praised Aureole.

A recipient of 1997 and 1998 James Beard awards and the 1996 Restaurants and Institutions Ivy Award, he is the author of *Great American Food* and *Charlie Palmer's Casual Cooking.*

STEVEN PICKER, executive chef and owner of Good, in New York's Greenwich Village, is a master of American comfort cooking, often with a twist. His wide culinary experience includes restaurants from Woods to Le Bernardin, from the casual Quilted Giraffe to the elegant catering of Glorious Food. Steven's food combines hearty rustic flavors with a sophisticated visual edge. His dishes meld elements from a broad array of cuisines but feature a uniquely American approach.

DON PINTABONA has been executive chef of New York's Tribeca Grill since its opening in 1990. After graduating from the Culinary Institute of America in 1982, he began a worldwide odyssey that would take him to more than thirty countries and into several renowned kitchens, including Michelin three-star Georges Blanc in France, Gentille Alouete in Osaka, Japan, and the River Café and Aureole in New York City.

Don's food has been featured in *Gourmet, Bon Appétit,* and *GQ,* among many other publications, and he has appeared on numerous television programs. He is the author of *The Tribeca Grill Cookbook* and is one of the five members of the Continental Airlines' Congress of Chefs.

DEBRA PONZEK, chef and owner of Aux Délices, a gourmet prepared foods shop with two branches in Greenwich, Connecticut, has received accolades for her innovative and subtle Provençal-inspired cuisine. Her early interest in cooking was nurtured by her mother and grandmother, but it wasn't until Debra was an engineering student at Boston University that she decided to pursue a career as a chef. She enrolled in the Culinary Institute of America and, after graduating in 1984, worked in top New Jersey restaurants. She was hired by Drew Nieporent as sous-chef at Montrachet, in Manhattan, and soon was promoted to chef, a position she held for seven years. Under her stewardship, Montrachet earned three consecutive three-star reviews from *The New York Times*.

Among her many honors, Debra was named a *Food & Wine* magazine Best New Chef of 1990 and a James Beard Foundation Rising Star Chef of the Year in 1991. She was the first American to receive the prestigious Moreau Award for culinary excellence from the Frederick Wildman and Sons Company. Debra is the author of *French Food/American Accent: Debra Ponzek's Spirited Cuisine.*

ALEX PORTER is executive chef at Norma's in New York's Le Parker Meridien Hotel. Treating breakfast as a dining experience, Alex has added new twists to old breakfast favorites. Recently he has rethought classic lunch items as well, as illustrated by his recipe for macaroni and cheese. A graduate of Colchester Avenue Catering College in Cardiff, Wales, Alex is a tireless supporter of City Harvest, working to feed the homeless of New York City.

NORA POUILLON is chef and owner of Nora—the first certified organic restaurant in the country—and Asia Nora, both in Washington, D.C. Born in Vienna, she moved to the United States in 1965 and operated a catering business and a cooking school before opening her first restaurant.

Chef Pouillon has consulted and developed products for Fresh Fields Wholefoods Market and Walnut Acres. She is a founding member of Chefs' Collaborative 2000 and was a leading spokesperson for the NRDC/SeaWeb "Give North Atlantic Swordfish a Break" campaign. She serves on the board of Women Chefs and Restaurateurs (WCR); on the NFAM International Committee on Alternative and Complementary Medicine; and is a member of Les Dames d'Escoffier and the American Institute of Food and Wine. Nora speaks nationally on her pioneering efforts in the organic food industry and is active in promoting a healthy and sustainable lifestyle.

Her cookbook, *Cooking with Nora,* was a finalist for the Julia Child awards for First Book. Nora was awarded the Chef of the Year Award of Excellence by the International Association of Culinary Professionals (IACP) and was chosen as one of the dozen "power chefs" in Washington by *The Washington Post.* Restaurant Nora is consistently in the *Zagat's* Top 10 and received a four-star rating from *Mobil Travel Guide 2001.*

ILENE ROSEN, in her first professional job in the food industry, as savory chef of City Bakery in New York City, has established herself as a fearless new talent. Ilene is possessed by the bounty of the Union Square greenmarket, and she routinely stalks New York's Chinatown with fervor and joy, in search of new foods to work with. She takes exotic as well as familiar ingredients and cooks clear, distinct, assured foods that have won her a loyal and growing following in downtown Manhattan.

BARBARA SHINN AND DAVID PAGE, owners of Home Restaurant and Shinn Vineyard, were born and raised in the Midwest and met in California in 1988, while David was cooking at the Dakota Grill and Barbara was earning her M.F.A. In the Bay Area, David cooked at Masa's, Postrio, and Café Americain. They moved to New York City in 1990 and quickly immersed themselves in its culinary community. In 1993, they opened Home, a small West Village restaurant with a local American menu that includes many wines from the North Fork of Long Island. In 2000, they planted their own twenty-two-acre vineyard on the North Fork, specializing in Merlot, and plan to produce small lots of high-quality handcrafted wines. They are the authors of *Recipes from Home.*

KATY SPARKS, executive chef at Quilty's, in New York City's SoHo, is the child of a Vermont professor who dabbled in cattle and chickens, and whose family vacations were planned around dining destinations. After studying linguistics, Katy graduated from Johnson and Wales University in 1986, at the top of her class.

She cooked at Campagne, in Seattle, and the Quilted Giraffe, in New York City, before moving to

Mesa Grill and Bolo, where chef Bobby Flay became her mentor. She then worked with chef Erika Gilmore at Kokachin, moved briefly to Solstice, and finally settled happily at Quilty's.

Katy has been named one of the Ten Best New Chefs of 1998 by *Food & Wine* magazine and a Rising Star Chef by both *Wine Spectator* and *Restaurant Hospitality* magazines. Her unique style—"Katycuisine"—is as varied as the seasons of the year and as exciting as the ethnic richness of New York.

ALLEN SUSSER established Chef Allen's Restaurant in Miami in 1986. After earning degrees from New York City Technical College and Le Cordon Bleu, he worked at the Bristol Hotel in Paris and went on to other kitchens in Florida and New York, most notably that of Le Cirque. His highly praised cuisine encompasses the foods, cultures, and techniques of the Mediterranean, the Americas, Asia, and India. Among his many honors: Honorary Doctor of Culinary Arts, Johnson and Wales University; National Advisory Board, James Beard Foundation; *Gourmet* magazine's Top Table in South Florida, 2000; Best Chef: Southeast, James Beard Foundation, 1994; Number one restaurant for Food and Most Popular in Miami, 1999 *Zagat Survey;* and National Board of Directors, American Institute of Food and Wine. He is the author of *New World Cuisine and Cookery* and *The Great Citrus Book.*

ALAN TARDI, chef-owner of Follonico in New York City, studied music at the University of Illinois and the San Francisco Conservatory and attended the New School for Social Research in New York. He cooked at Chanterelle; Ristorante La Chiusa in Montefollonico, Italy; Restaurant Lafayette; and Le Madri (as executive chef). In 1992, he opened the critically acclaimed Follonico. Alan is a strong supporter of Chefs' Collaborative 2000, the Slow Food movement, and the American Institute of Food and Wine, and is an active member of New York City Greenmarket's Farmer-Consumer Advisory Committee. He has taught cooking classes in New York, served frequently on juries at the French Culinary Institute, and acted as guest chef-instructor at the Culinary Institute of America. Alan has written articles for the journals *Fine Cooking* and *Wine and Spirits.*

JANOS WILDER, chef-owner of Janos and J Bar in Tucson, Arizona, earned a degree in political science from the University of California, Berkeley. He moved to Boulder, Colorado, and worked his way up from cook to sous-chef to chef at the city's top restaurants. He was chef at the Gold Hill Inn in Gold Hill,

Colorado, and then moved to Le Mirage in Santa Fe, New Mexico, before heading to France to work in the Bordeaux restaurants La Reserve and La Duberne. In 1983, Janos and his wife, Rebecca, opened Janos on the grounds of the Tucson Museum of Art (since moved to the Westin La Paloma Resort), and in 1998, they opened the casual J Bar restaurant.

Chef Wilder was inducted into the Scottsdale Culinary Hall of Fame in 1993 and was named Best Chef: Southwest by the James Beard Foundation in May 2000. He is the author of *Janos: Recipes and Tales from a Southwest Restaurant.*

JOYCE WILDER is a native San Franciscan who raised her family (including her son, chef Janos Wilder) on the midpeninsula. A great host and accomplished home cook, Mrs. Wilder is inspired by cookbooks, magazines, and her extensive travels. She has created numerous recipes that have become part of her family's culinary traditions, and her recipe for macaroni and cheese was a household favorite when her children were young.

JOSEPH WREDE, a native of Phoenix, Arizona, and the chef and co-owner of Joseph's Table in Taos, New Mexico, was voted one of America's Ten Best New Chefs of 2000 by *Food & Wine* magazine. He is a graduate of Peter Kump's New York Cooking School and a cum laude graduate of Regis College in Colorado. Before working at Aubergine Café and Today's Gourmet, both in Denver, Colorado, he "worked in one bad restaurant after another in every conceivable capacity." Joseph's food is about adventure, availability, and mood, and he is known for his skillful combinations of ingredients.

INDEX

INDEX

INDEX

INDEX

INDEX

ABOUT THE AUTHOR

JOAN SCHWARTZ is a graduate of Rutgers University and received an M.A. from the University of Chicago. She has worked as an editor for the University of Chicago Press, Columbia University Press, Macmillan Publishing Company, and The Free Press. She is an avid reader, writer, and cook, and is the coauthor of many acclaimed books, including Bobby Flay's *Boy Meets Grill* and *From My Kitchen to Your Table* and Joel Patraker's *The Greenmarket Cookbook*. Joan and her husband divide their time between Westchester and New York City, and have three grown children.